S0-CPR-554

MARCO POLO'S
ADVENTURES IN CHINA

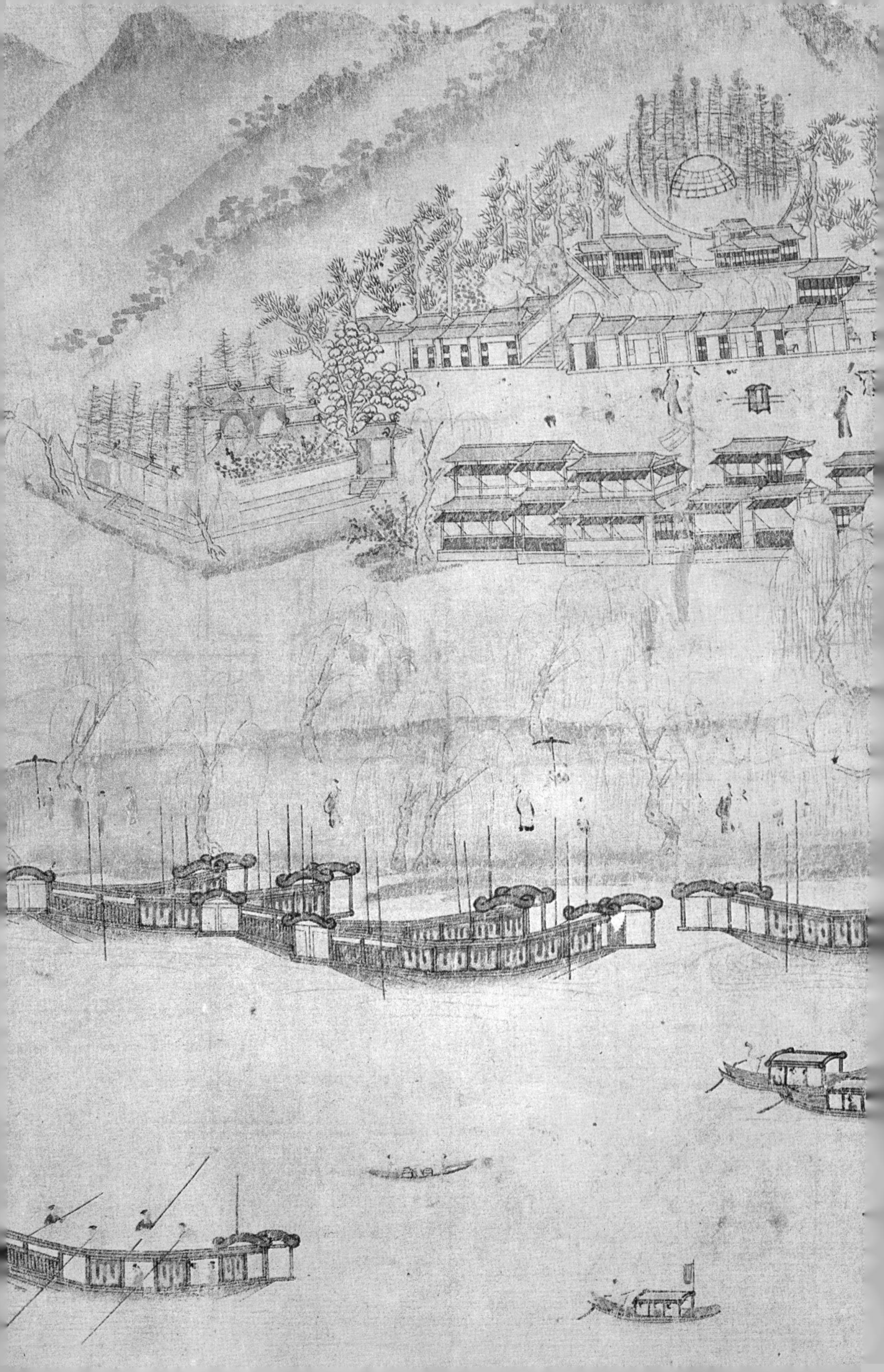

There are six new HORIZON CARAVEL BOOKS published each year. The titles now available are:

MARCO POLO'S ADVENTURES IN CHINA
SHAKESPEARE'S ENGLAND
CAPTAIN COOK AND THE SOUTH PACIFIC
THE SEARCH FOR EARLY MAN
JOAN OF ARC
EXPLORATION OF AFRICA
NELSON AND THE AGE OF FIGHTING SAIL
ALEXANDER THE GREAT
RUSSIA UNDER THE CZARS
HEROES OF POLAR EXPLORATION
KNIGHTS OF THE CRUSADES

American Heritage also publishes AMERICAN HERITAGE JUNIOR LIBRARY books, a similar series on American history. The titles now available are:

THE ERIE CANAL
THE MANY WORLDS OF BENJAMIN FRANKLIN
COMMODORE PERRY IN JAPAN
THE BATTLE OF GETTYSBURG
ANDREW JACKSON, SOLDIER AND STATESMAN
ADVENTURES IN THE WILDERNESS
LEXINGTON, CONCORD AND BUNKER HILL
CLIPPER SHIPS AND CAPTAINS
D-DAY, THE INVASION OF EUROPE
WESTWARD ON THE OREGON TRAIL
THE FRENCH AND INDIAN WARS
GREAT DAYS OF THE CIRCUS
STEAMBOATS ON THE MISSISSIPPI
COWBOYS AND CATTLE COUNTRY
TEXAS AND THE WAR WITH MEXICO
THE PILGRIMS AND PLYMOUTH COLONY
THE CALIFORNIA GOLD RUSH
PIRATES OF THE SPANISH MAIN
TRAPPERS AND MOUNTAIN MEN
MEN OF SCIENCE AND INVENTION
NAVAL BATTLES AND HEROES
THOMAS JEFFERSON AND HIS WORLD
DISCOVERERS OF THE NEW WORLD
RAILROADS IN THE DAYS OF STEAM
INDIANS OF THE PLAINS
THE STORY OF YANKEE WHALING

COVER: *In the China of Marco Polo, dragons were considered creatures of good fortune. The royal family traditionally adopted a five-clawed dragon, like this one, for its badge.*
PAINTING BY ISADORE SELTZER

ENDSHEETS: *The Chinese city that impressed Marco most was Kinsai, now Hangchow. Shown here are barges on the city's lake and the generous market place lined with shops.*
COURTESY OF THE SMITHSONIAN INSTITUTION, FREER GALLERY OF ART

TITLE PAGE: *This woodcut of "Marco Paulo" was in the first Spanish edition of his book.*
Il Milione, BENEDETTO, 1928

A HORIZON CARAVEL BOOK

MARCO POLO'S
ADVENTURES IN CHINA

By the Editors of

HORIZON MAGAZINE

Author

MILTON RUGOFF

Consultant

L. CARRINGTON GOODRICH

Professor Emeritus of Chinese, Columbia University

ILLUSTRATED WITH PAINTINGS, MAPS,
AND ILLUMINATIONS, MANY OF THE PERIOD

Published by American Heritage Publishing Co., Inc.
Book Trade and Institutional Distribution by
Harper & Row

FIRST EDITION

Library of Congress Catalogue Card Number: 64-14324

BODLEIAN LIBRARY, OXFORD

honnoure par la voie alant et tournant de tout ce que
il savoient commander. Ci dit le xiiij. chapitre
Comment messire nicole et messire mafe et marc
alerent devant le grant Caan o lres dele pape

Que vous en diroie. Quant li doi fre
res et marc furent venu en cele grant
cite, si sen alerent au maistre palais.
la ou il troverent le grant seignour
a mult grant compaignie de barons.
Il sagenoullierent devant lui, et sumelierent tant
comme il porent le seignour les fist drecier en estant
et les recut mult honnourablement et leur fist

FOREWORD

"The multitude of tigers makes traveling dangerous unless a number of persons go in company. . . . Many come here to have their bodies ornamented by puncturing with needles. . . . the annual revenue to His Majesty amounted to 16,800,000 ducats." With such sharp and richly descriptive phrases the young Venetian traveler Marco Polo wrote of the journey he and his father and uncle made to the court of Kublai Khan in China between the years 1271 and 1295.

That journey changed the history of Europe just as decisively as did the explorations of Christopher Columbus two centuries later. Indeed, Columbus was trying to find the lands so enticingly described by Marco Polo. After Marco's voyage, no well-read European could believe that the world was cramped or impoverished; Marco had demonstrated that it was vast, brimming with adventure, and abounding with wealth.

China in the thirteenth century was unmistakably richer and more civilized than Europe; its art (as seen in the pages of this book) was infinitely more skilled than contemporary European works. Yet the reason Marco could journey overland to China and see its treasures was that all Asia at that time was ruled by the fierce Mongol warriors of the Great Khan—men who despite their love of combat were tolerant of foreigners. Kublai himself was intensely curious about the lands of the West and regarded Marco's uncle and father as his personal envoys to the pope.

The Great Khan hoped that the Polos' journey would promote world harmony, or at least more vigorous trade. Yet a wholly different result came to pass. Marco Polo made it possible for men in his time to see beyond their narrow medieval world; to them and to future generations he bequeathed the spirit of exploration.

THE EDITORS

METROPOLITAN MUSEUM OF ART, FLETCHER FUND, 1934

The ivory carving above of a dragon-borne Buddha was made in China about the time of the Polos' journey. The illumination at left for a French manuscript of 1400 shows the Polos giving the Great Khan a letter from the pope.

A princess is being carted across a river in this painting. The Chinese artist pictured the Mongols who are escorting her as ruffians.

CONTENTS

Das ist der edel Ritter · Marcho polo von
Venedig der grost landtfarer · der vns beschreibt die grossen wunder der welt
die er selber gesehen hat · Von dem aufgang
pis zu dem nidergang der sunnen · der gleichen vor nicht meer gehort seyn

I

MARCO'S BOOK

Day after day during the years 1297 and 1298 a strange performance took place in the jail in Genoa where high-ranking prisoners of war were kept. One of the prisoners, a sturdy man in his early forties, told of his experiences while another copied them down. Not only were other prisoners and the jailers gathered about, but occasionally the leading citizens of Genoa came to listen. For the story the man told was the most fascinating that any of them had ever heard—and doubly so because every word of it, he claimed, was true.

He told how he had traveled for almost twenty-five years in strange places, among unheard-of peoples thousands of miles to the east. His audience listened in amazement as he described the dazzling gold and silver pagodas of Burma, the black magic of the wizards of Kashmir, the shark charmers who protected the pearl divers of Ceylon, and the cannibals of Sumatra. Most astonishing were his tales of the country farthest to the east, the land called Cathay. He spoke of it as the greatest empire that had ever been known, with the most people and wealth and the most powerful emperor in all of history.

ESCORIAL LIBRARY, SPAIN

At first the listeners shook their heads in disbelief, but as the speaker, consulting his notes, gave facts and figures and countless details, they were overwhelmed. Surely, they thought, this will be the most marvelous travel story ever put on paper.

And so it was. The man they listened to was Marco Polo, respectfully known as Messer Marco, a merchant of Venice, and the book he dictated was *Description of the World*, or, as it later came to be known in English, *The Trav-*

The book that Marco Polo dictated in prison appeared in many forms. At left is the title page of the first printed edition (1477) with a drawing of Marco. The capital letter above is from an earlier manuscript version.

With rotting floor boards and dark walls, this cell in Venice's ducal palace became a virtual chamber of horrors for the hapless souls who were sentenced to isolation there.

SOPRINTENDENZA MONUMENTI VENEZIA

els of Marco Polo. He had been a prisoner of war for nearly three years, having been captured in a sea battle between the Genoese and the Venetians, probably around 1296.

At last a truce was declared between Genoa and Venice in 1299, and Marco Polo was released. Joyfully he went home, bearing his manuscript. But the people who had scoffed at his stories when he first returned from his travels were still reluctant to believe him. Even after his manuscript began to be widely copied, most readers regarded him as a mere teller of tall tales. How could anyone believe a man who told of a city so large that it had 12,000 bridges, of winds so hot they suffocated men and turned their bodies to dust, of black stones (coal) and a liquid (petroleum) that burned, of a kind of pony express with 10,000 stations and 200,000 horses, and of a land to the north where it was night all winter and day all summer?

Only a handful of people paid heed. But that handful included a few geographers, map makers, and explorers. They took note of his descriptions of people and places and his estimates of distances. But most of all they were fascinated by his stories of the gold and spices he had seen in the royal courts and the cities of the East. In an age when there was no way to preserve food, or to make it palatable after it had been kept, except by spicing it lavishly, spices

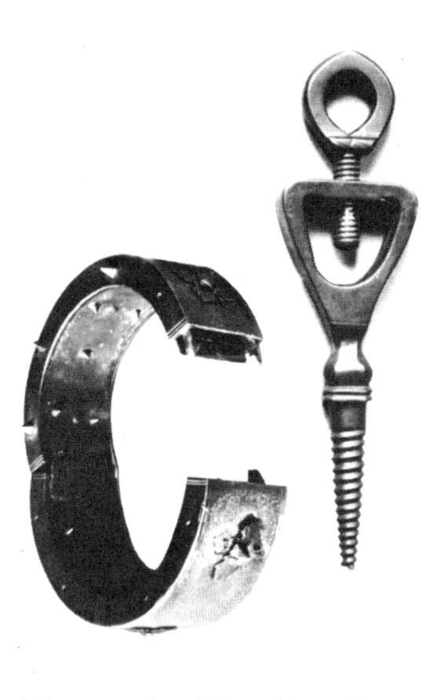

were precious. As for gold, it was still the best international currency. So Marco's stories spurred men's hopes and fed their dreams.

Among the dreamers of a later period was a sea captain from Genoa by the name of Christopher Columbus. His dream was that he might reach the lands of spices and gold by sailing westward. One of the maps he studied had been sent to him in 1474 by the Italian geographer Toscanelli, who had based his idea of the locations of Zipangu (Japan) and the Indies on Marco Polo's descriptions. Columbus himself had read Marco's *Travels* with great care. One of the most interesting documents in the history of exploration is a Latin edition of Marco's book (now in Seville) with notes by Columbus in the margins of seventy pages.

The Travels of Marco Polo surely stimulated Columbus' ambitions and imagination more than any other single book.

A few other thoughtful men came to realize that Marco had brought back from Asia something even more valuable

TEXT CONTINUED ON PAGE 16

The engraving below shows the variety of punishments once inflicted on prisoners, men whose lives ended in pain and agony. Two medieval torture instruments, a thumbscrew and an iron collar, appear above.

MUSEO CORRER, VENICE

BIBLIOTECA NAZIONALE, FLORENCE

Marco Polo's concept of Asian geography is included in the football-shaped map above on which Europe is at left, China at right. Painted in 1457,

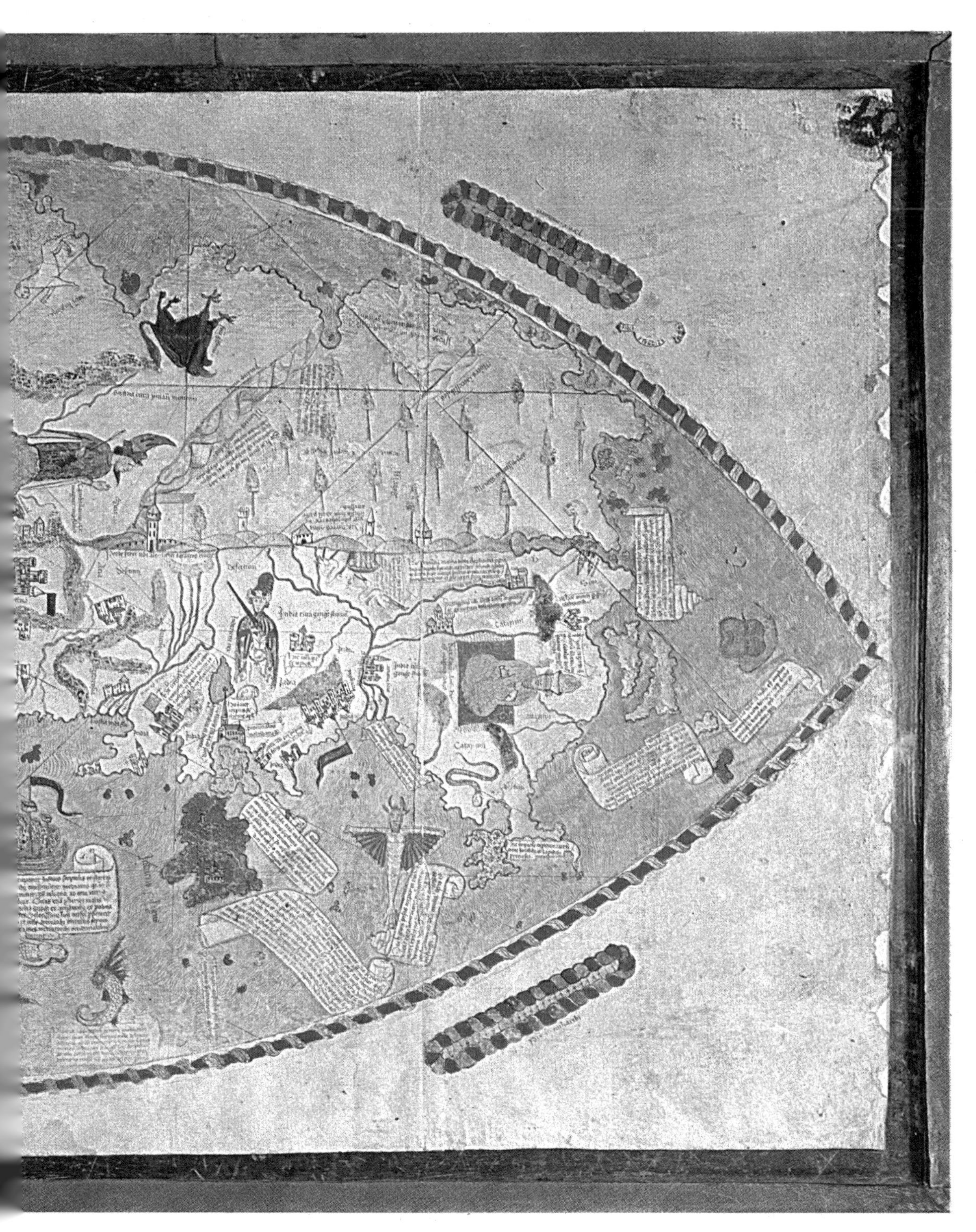

this view of the world was scarcely amended until Columbus sailed westward, hoping to reach Asia that way, and accidentally discovered America.

TEXT CONTINUED FROM PAGE 13

than spices and gold—a knowledge of other civilizations and other people. Where such later discoverers as Columbus and Cook often merely touched the shores of unknown lands, Marco Polo described a continent and all that was in it.

He brought back a wealth of information not only on mountains and deserts, on goods, crafts, and inventions, but on governments and religions and customs. He described individuals and groups from whom Europeans could learn much: the Hindu Brahmans, who were the soul of honor; the Chinese, who treasured learning and art; an emperor, Kublai Khan, who tolerated all religions; the Buddhists, whose founder was a model of holiness; and the yogis, who would not hurt a living thing.

Marco Polo's manuscript, circulating throughout Europe, was one of the lamps that lit the way to modern learning and to that great rebirth of interest in the world and its peoples that we call the Renaissance.

ROYAL LIBRARY, STOCKHOLM

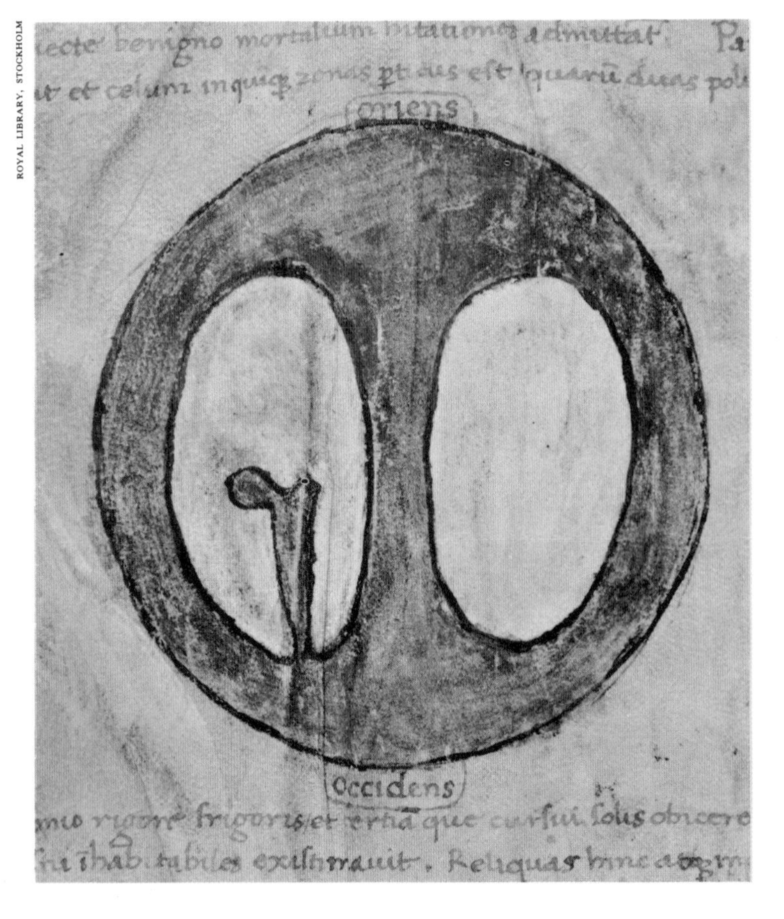

The only world map to appear in a manuscript version of Marco's book was the strange globe at left: two hemispheres floating in an ocean. The Northern Hemisphere (the one on the left) was pictured as split by the Mediterranean plus the Nile and Don rivers. At right is a page from a Latin edition of the book; the marginal comments, including a crudely drawn hand, were probably made by Columbus before he sailed.

tissimũ hꝫ qui nulli tributariꝰ ẽ Hoĩes insule ydolatre sũt
et oẽs nude ãbulant mares et femine ẜ quilibꝫ verecũda
opit pãno vno Nullũ bladũ hñt excepto riso Carnibꝰ ri
so et lacte viuũt habũdanciã hñt seminũ solũmõ de quibꝰ
oleũ faciũt hñt hiricios meliores mũdi qui ibi crescũt Vi
nũ eciã hñt de arboribꝰ de quibꝰ dcm̃ ẽ suꝑ in regno sama-
rã In hac isula lapides ꝑciosi iueniũt qui dicũt Rubini
qui i regionibꝰ alijs nõ inueniũt vel hñt. Multi eni eciã
saphiri et topacij et amatiste ibi sunt multiqꝫ alij lapides ꝑ
ciosi Rex huius insule habet pulchriorẽ rubinũ qui vnq̃
fuit visus in hoc mũdo habet enim vniꝰ palme longitudi-
nẽ et ad mensurã grossiciei brachij hoĩs Est ãt splendidꝰ
suꝑ modũ omni macula carens adeo vt ignis ardens vide
atur esse Magnꝰ kaam Cublay nuncios suos direxit ad
illũ rogans vt prefatũ lapidẽ illi donaret et ipe donaret ei
valorẽ vnius ciuitatis Qui rñdit q lapis ille suoꝝ erat añ
cessorũ nulli eũ vnq̃ homini daret Huiꝰ insule hoĩes bel
licosi non sunt sed valde viles Quando autẽ bella cũ aliq̃
bus habent de alienis ꝑtibus stipendiarios vocant et spe
cialiter sarracenos

hic inveniũt rubi(ni) / saphiri / topaci / hic ẽ Rubinũ / unius palmi / splendens (mirabili

De regno maabar Capitulũ xxiij.

Ultra insulã seylã ad miliaria xl iuenit maabar q̃ ma-
ior india nũcupat Nõ aũt ẽ insula ẜ terra firma. In
hac ꝓuincia quinqꝫ reges sũt Prouicia ẽ nobilissiã et ditis
sima suꝑ modũ In ꝑmo huiꝰ ꝓuicie rex ẽ noiẽ Sendeba
i quo regno sũt margarite i copia maxiã In mari eni huiꝰ
ꝓuincie ẽ maris brachiũ seu sinus int firmã terrã et insulã
q̃dã vbi nõ est aquaꝝ ꝓfũditas vltra decem vel duodeci
passus et alicubi vltra duos Ibi inueniũt margarite suꝑ
dcẽ Mercatores eni diuersi societates adinuicẽ faciunt ⁊
hñt naues magnas et ꝑuas hoĩesqꝫ cõducunt qui descen-
dũt ad ꝓfundũ aquarũ et capiunt cõchilia in quibus sunt

hic inveniẽt margarite ĩ copia max / mare badosũ / naves magnas

PHOTO BY FIORENTINI

Four bronze horses, brought to Venice after the sack of Constantinople in 1204, stand atop the main entrance to the Church of St. Mark. These relics, each weighing one ton, remain as mementos of Venice's former might.

II

VENICE

A winged lion, emblem of Venice's patron saint, Saint Mark, was the ensign of the Venetian republic.

The Venice in which Marco Polo grew up was a place to stir the blood and excite a hundred dreams in the mind of a boy. As late as A.D. 500 it had been only a cluster of marshy islands huddling in a lagoon off the northern shores of the Adriatic and occupied mainly by hardy fisherfolk. But by the year of Marco's birth, 1254, Venice had become Queen of the Adriatic, an enchanted, canal-laced city floating magically on the sea, heart of the greatest mercantile empire the world had ever seen.

Into its crowded wharves from dawn to dusk came sailing ships laden with exotic wares—ivory, spices, slaves—from far-off places. Along its network of canals, some barely a dozen feet wide, others broad as rivers, fleets of bright gondolas glided. Over the arcs of its hundreds of bridges and through its many squares passed men from every country of Europe and from Asia Minor and North Africa. Dressed in colorful garb and jabbering in unfamiliar tongues, they trailed an aura of mysterious and exciting places.

Venice flourished because its location established it as the great trading center between East and West. Close to the heart of Europe, it was still not too far by sailing ship from the eastern Mediterranean. Goods from India, Persia, Arabia, and areas bordering the Caspian Sea came by caravan to Constantinople, or to Acre and other ports of the eastern Mediterranean, and then were funneled up the Adriatic to Venice. Similarly, merchandise poured into Venice from the cities of France, the Low Countries, England, and Central Europe. It came by pack horse over Alpine passes or by galley around Spain. Much of it was then shipped out again across the seas to the ports of the eastern Mediterranean.

The Venetian traders, such as those Shakespeare later portrayed in *The Merchant of Venice*, were avaricious men who missed no opportunity to make money. While much of Europe lay mired in poverty and pestilence or was en-

TEXT CONTINUED ON PAGE 22

WALTERS ART GALLERY, BALTIMORE

The gateway to Venice from the Adriatic Sea is seen here as a string of fortresses protecting the is

Venice appears dotted with tall spires in this eighteenth-century copy of an Arab map made in 1657.

TEXT CONTINUED FROM PAGE 19
tangled in wars, Venice remained at peace—except with Genoa—and concentrated on commerce. While Europe's feudal kings and barons scorned trade as beneath their dignity, but did not hesitate to rob one another, Venetian merchants traded all across Europe. They sailed up the larger rivers, including the whole length of the Danube. They called at every Atlantic port from Gibraltar to the North Sea. Annually, for example, several vessels would stop at English ports and exchange cargoes of spices for wool, which the Venetians would then bring back to the weavers of Florence, Lucca, and Genoa. On the high seas, pirates were a constant threat, and merchants sailed in armed galleys for protection. In many lands, they were often in danger from greedy barons, and they even took troupes of musicians, acrobats, and clowns with them in order to charm these noblemen into letting them do business.

To the east, Venetian merchants and their rivals from Genoa established commercial colonies in Ayas, a Mediterranean port in Armenia, and in Constantinople. Groups of merchants could be found around the Black Sea, especially in the Crimea, and as far east as Bukhara in western Asia.

They had made great fortunes even out of the Crusades. For one hundred and fifty years before Marco's time, countless Europeans had joined in armies sworn to drive the Moslems out of the Holy Land. Over the years the Crusaders had used Venice as the place to gather and to get galleys, food, arms, and armor before they set sail for Jerusalem. The Venetians had taken full advantage of this literally golden opportunity. While acting as though they were serving Christianity, they had served their own fortunes even more.

The Fourth Crusade, which began in 1202, was their greatest success, and their greatest shame. When the Crusaders, assembled in Venice, were unable to pay for their supplies, the Venetians offered to furnish troops, equipment, and transportation—for which they would be repaid with the spoils of future conquests. What the Venetians desired was to have the Crusaders join them in assaulting Constantinople. This great city, capital of the wealthy Byzantine Empire, was a commercial rival to Venice's mercantile

Crusaders and their Venetian allies storm Constantinople in a painting by Domenico Tintoretto. At left soldiers scale the walls; other men are being swung to the towers by the ships' booms. Before the gate stands an array of churchmen, who hoped to make the city submit to the authority of Rome.

PALAZZO DUCALE, VENICE: PHOTO BY BOHM

These pictures were drawn to illustrate arithmetic problems in a Venetian trader's textbook of the fourteenth century. The merchants meeting for lunch (right) pose a problem relating to distance, rate, and time. The two galleys shown below illustrate the question of how to divide cargo fairly if many traders happen to own interests in it.

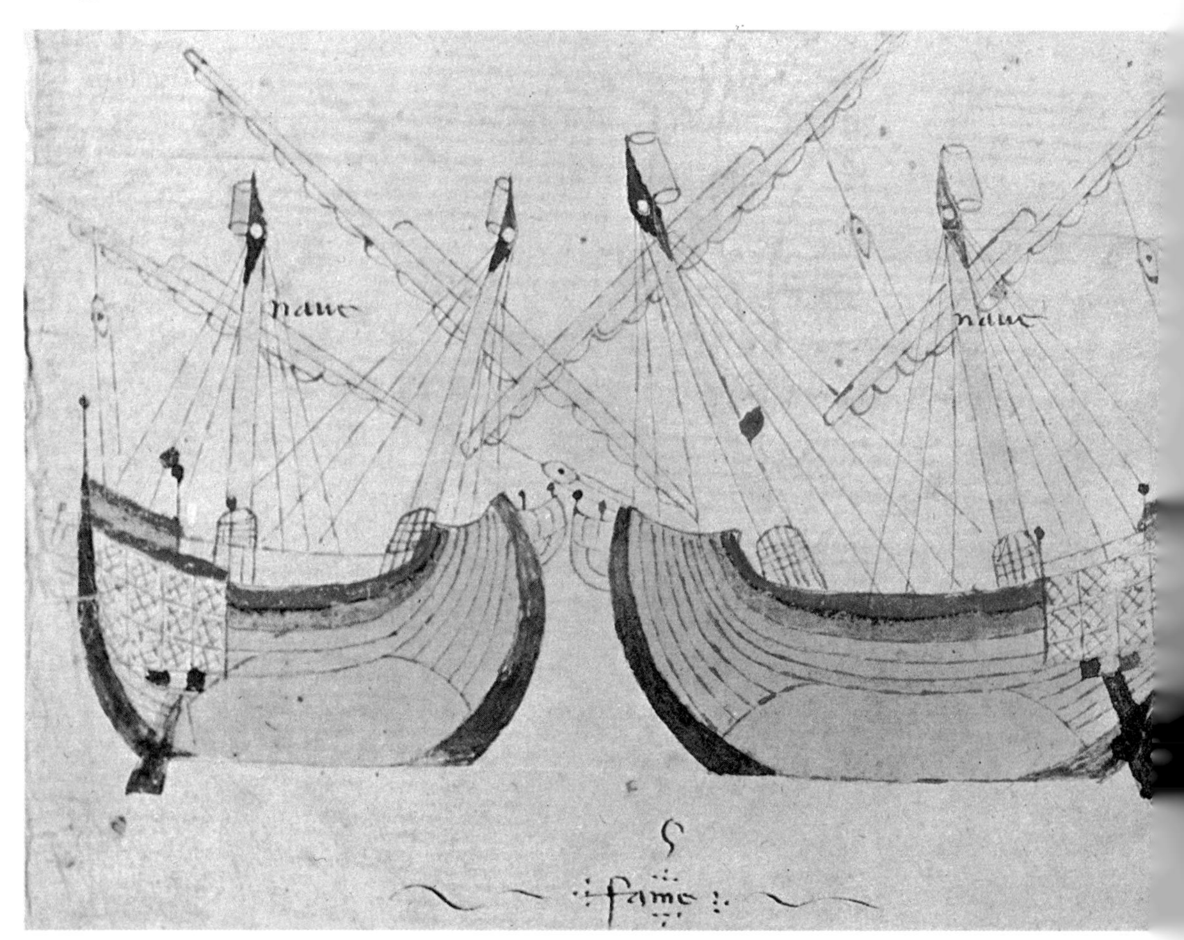

power. The Venetians hoped to destroy the supremacy of Constantinople and also to plunder its fabulous riches.

The attack on Constantinople by the combined forces of the zealous Crusaders and the greedy Venetians was ferocious and devastating. In sacking the city, the Venetians carried off booty of every kind, including the four bronze horses that to this day decorate the face of Venice's celebrated Church of St. Mark. Even more important, they took over those sections of the fallen Byzantine Empire that would aid their maritime power and even claimed a quarter in Constantinople itself. Thus the wealth and power of Venice came from its fortunate location between East and West, from the Crusaders and pilgrims who passed through it, and from its venturesome and sometimes ruthless merchants.

Among the more ambitious merchants of mid thirteenth century Venice were Nicolo Polo and his brother Maffeo. Nicolo's son Marco was born shortly before the two brothers set off on a long journey. While Nicolo was away, Marco's mother died, and the boy probably went to live with an aunt.

Since the average Venetian youth spent little time in school, Marco was free to wander about the city, and he came to know it as only a curious boy could.

At the heart of Venice was the wonderfully spacious Piazza San Marco, St. Mark's Square, bounded on three sides by busy shops and markets and on the fourth by the already famous church with its fanciful pointed arches and mosquelike domes. Inside, the old church was cool and mysteriously dim, filled with the fumes of incense and the chanting of priests. The walls were covered with rich mosaics of biblical incidents, and behind the high altar was the Pala d'Oro, a screen of gold, silver, and enamel encrusted with almost three thousand pearls, rubies, emeralds, and other gems.

In front of the church were the city's most fascinating people, who moved through the square in an endless river of contrasts. There were nobles and rich men, the latter truly merchant princes who were already building the palaces that would make the Grand Canal a fantasy of water-borne grace and opulence. There were occasional beggars and lepers, and sweeping haughtily past them were perfumed gallants. There were fashionable women who wore silks and brocades and teetered along through the mud of the unpaved streets on stiltlike clogs so dangerously high (some were three feet tall) that they were later prohibited. There

SAN MARCO, VENICE: PHOTO BY ALINARI

Four shipwrights, bodies contorted by their labors, are at work on a tiny boat in this carved marble relief that is in St. Mark's Church.

were pickpockets and gamblers. There were Jews, mostly traders, doctors, and moneylenders, who were sometimes tolerated and sometimes expelled, but always restricted. There were dark-skinned sailors from Ethiopia, Egypt, and Arabia, and big, blond men from the Baltic states and Germany. And there were slaves—usually young girls—Tartar, Russian, Turkish, African. The slave trade was inhuman, but Venetian and other Italian merchants found it highly profitable, for a pretty girl might fetch as much as four thousand dollars at an auction. Marco Polo himself brought back from his Oriental travels a Tartar slave, Peter, but Marco's will provided that the slave should be freed.

Many of the activities of Venetian life went on out-of-doors, and Marco became familiar with some astonishing spectacles—a few horrible, a few colorful and exciting. The most dreadful was the barbaric punishment of criminals—pickpockets whose hands were cut off, thieves with their eyes torn out, and murderers who were decapitated or burned or sometimes even quartered alive. Or for a minor offense a man might be thrust into a cage suspended from the side of the main bell tower in St. Mark's Square where any passer-by could jeer at him.

BIBLIOTECA MARCIANA, VENICE

A clerical procession pauses before the Church of St. Mark in this picture from a medieval manuscript.

In contrast to these cruelties were the festivals, the pageants, and the processions on saints' days. The most unforgettable by far was the pageant on Ascension Day when the city celebrated—as it still does— its "wedding with the sea." For this occasion a host of gondolas and other vessels, all gaily bedecked, gathered on the glittering water off St. Mark's. Led by the doge, or ruler, in his resplendent barge, they made their way toward Venice's outermost island, the Lido. As the vessels approached the island the doge rose, and dropping a golden ring into the water, cried, "We wed thee, O our Sea, in sign of true and perpetual dominion." Then for seven days there was a fair in St. Mark's Square in which wares from all over the world were shown, and along with it was much feasting and revelry. There was a good reason why the Venetians adored the sea; it was a great artery carrying trade, the lifeblood of the city, out to the remotest parts of the known world.

But the finest show of all was at the Arsenal. Turning out ships for the greatest merchant and military fleet in the world, the Arsenal was the key to the maritime power of Venice. And its artisans performed their tasks with a speed and efficiency that was the wonder of the world. Every shipyard procedure, from seasoning wood to equipping a vessel

N.F.G.C., VENICE

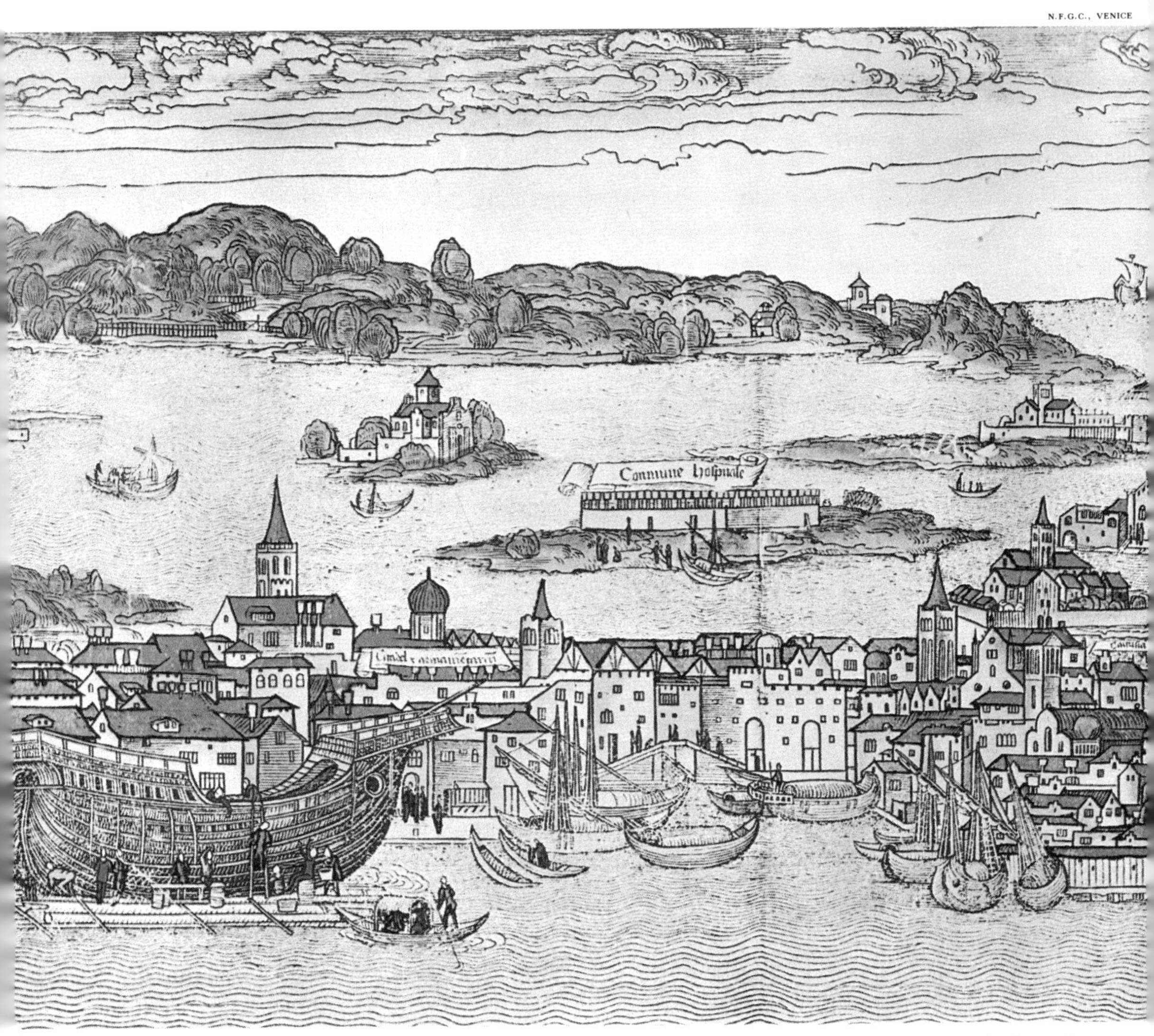

A half-finished vessel floats before the Arsenal shipyards where the Venetian merchant navy was built. This is a detail from an illustration in a book of 1486.

with anchors, sails, calking, and cannon, was so organized that a ship could be completed in one continuous series of steps. A later visitor to Venice, Pero Tafur, has left a wonderfully vivid description of the speed with which the hull of a war galley was completed during a visit he made to the Arsenal in 1436:

As one enters the gate there is a great street on either hand with the sea in the middle, and on one side are windows opening out of the houses of the Arsenal, and the same on the other side. And out came a galley towed by a boat, and from the windows they handed out to them, from one the cordage, from another the bread, from another the arms, from another the ballistas and mortars, and so from all sides everything that was required. And when the galley had reached the end of the street, all the men required were on board, together with the complement of oars, and she was equipped from end to end. In this manner there came out ten galleys, fully armed, between the hours of three and nine. I know not how to describe what I saw there, whether in the manner of its construction or in the management of the work-people, and I do not think there is anything finer in the world.

Like the shipyard craftsmen, all the artisans of the city were proud of their work, and their societies, called guilds, paraded grandly in civic ceremonies. One of the most celebrated of these was the pageant that took place in 1268 when Lorenzo Tiepolo was elected doge of Venice. First a fleet of galleys passed before the Doges' Palace, the sailors saluting the new head of state with songs and cheers. Then, their members marching two by two, came the guilds, each arrayed more sumptuously, more gorgeously, than the next. In the van were the master smiths, with banners flying and trumpets calling and with garlands on their heads. Then came the furriers in mantles of ermine, the master tailors in white robes with crimson stars, and the makers of cloth of

N.Y. PUBLIC LIBRARY, PRINTS DIVISION

Wrongdoers in medieval Venice were punished in St. Mark's Square. A man might be suspended in a cage from the bell tower (above). Or he could be tied between the pillars shown below and at left; they were brought back from the Holy Land.

N.F.G.C., VENICE

MUSEO CIVICO, PADUA

gold, all wearing cloth of gold. After these marched the master glassworkers clothed in fur-trimmed scarlet robes and bearing the exquisite flasks and goblets of their art. Following them were the lanternmakers, who as they passed released birds from their lanterns; and after them paraded goldsmiths with necklaces and garlands of gold and silver and precious stones. Each guild, accompanied by musicians, came bearing silver cups and flagons of wine. The celebration went on for a whole week.

Marco was fourteen when this pageant took place, old enough to remember its details for the rest of his life. The splendor of the celebration was typical of Venice in the last half of the thirteenth century—a great city that looked as much toward the East as toward the West. Wandering through this city, a young man as yet unconcerned with his future, Marco probably did not realize that his own destiny lay in the East. For the greatest event of his young life would prove to be the historic journey that his father and uncle were then making into Asia.

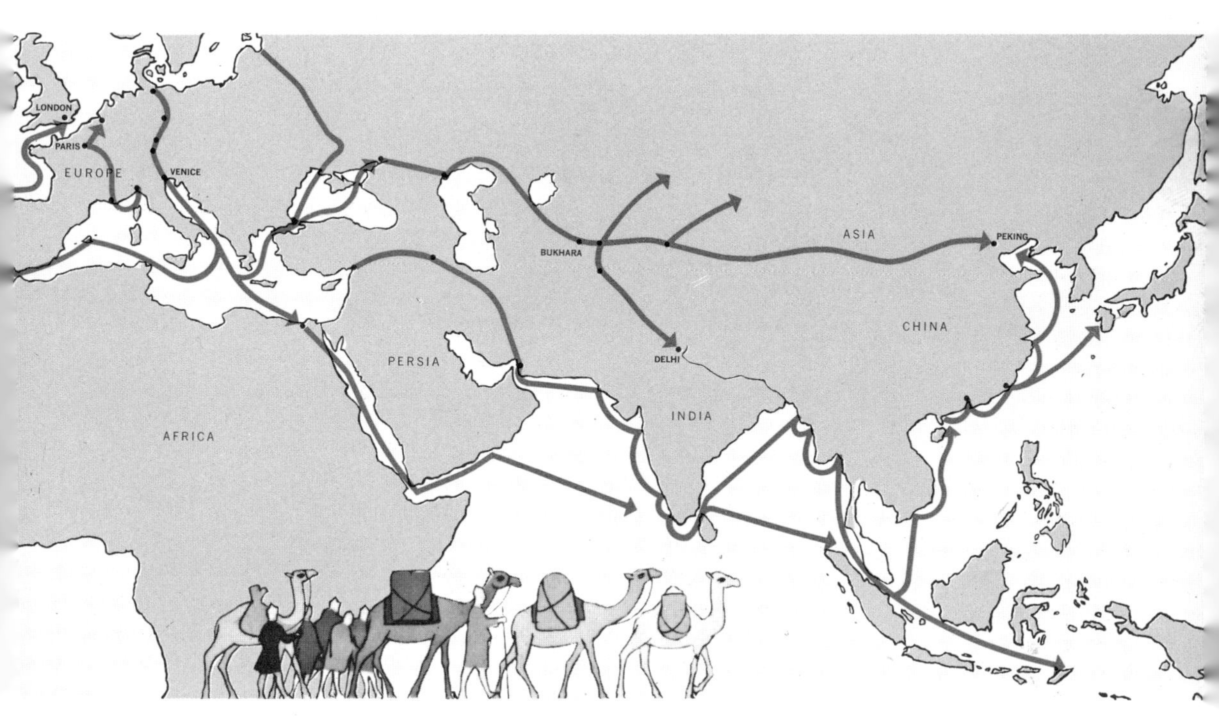

By the mid thirteenth century, Europe was beginning to look beyond its own boundaries. Traders and missionaries were bringing East and West into contact, and soon medieval trade routes to the East (above) carried steady traffic. Travelers had a choice of two main routes: the Great Silk Road by land across Central Asia or the long sea route south of Persia and India.

PHOTO BY SCALA

HICDEFERTvRC ORPvSSCIMARC

III

A PROMISE TO THE KHAN

When the brothers Nicolo and Maffeo Polo, merchants of Venice, set out in 1254, they intended to make an ordinary trading trip to Constantinople, where they had a branch of their business. Instead, they crossed the whole vast and unknown continent of Asia and were gone for fifteen years. Nicolo's son Marco was an infant when they left; he would be a young man by the time they returned.

The voyage to Constantinople usually took five or six weeks and could be a hard one, what with seasickness, poor food, and especially the pirates that roamed the seas. Loading the hold of their ship with a rich variety of merchandise, the brothers sailed southward through the Adriatic, rounded the southern tip of Greece, and made their way past fabled Troy and the Aegean Islands. Toward the end of their voyage they threaded the narrow strait called the Hellespont (now the Dardanelles) and at last dropped anchor in Constantinople's harbor.

From A.D. 330, when the Emperor Constantine had moved the capital of the Roman Empire to Byzantium—thereafter known as Constantinople—that city had been one of the wonders of the world. Robert de Clari, a Frenchman who took part in the Crusaders' siege of the city in 1204 and saw its treasures being plundered, declared:

> . . . there were so many rich vessels of gold and silver and cloth of gold and so many rich jewels that it was a fair marvel the great wealth that was brought there . . . And if anyone should recount to you the hundredth part of the richness and the beauty and the nobility that was found in the abbeys and in the churches and in the palaces . . . it would seem like a lie and you would not believe it.

Crafted of jewels and enamel, the panel at left is from the Pala d'Oro, the huge altar screen in St. Mark's Church. This section depicts a biblical scene: four men cross the sea in a vessel with a high bow and a forked stern.

In the fires that followed the pillaging of the city much of this wealth was laid waste. Fifty years later, at the time the Polo brothers reached Constantinople, the city had recovered most of its former trade. But many of its buildings were still in ruins or had long been stripped of their copper roofs, bronze ornaments, and tiles. A good many poor families had moved into the once finer districts, so that hovels often stood side by side with palaces. Despite its dilapidation, the city was still the greatest center of trade in the West and still had ten times the population of Venice. All the major caravan routes of Asia led to it; its excellent harbor was the most crowded in the eastern Mediterranean; and its currency was accepted everywhere. Its caravansaries and bazaars brought together Greeks and Turks, Egyptians and Genoese, Englishmen and Tartars, Armenians and Venetians. Here East and West, and Christian, Moslem, and Jew, met and mingled.

Nicolo and Maffeo Polo remained in Constantinople

Events from Nicolo and Maffeo's voyage are illustrated in a group of miniatures from a fourteenth-century manuscript. Below, the Polos and their entourage row into a Black Sea port. At right, having arrived in Constantinople, they visit Emperor Baldwin II.

about six years, carrying on a trade chiefly in precious stones. By that time they could see that a major struggle was in the making between the so-called Latin emperors, who were friendly to the Venetians, and a line of Greek rulers. So the brothers decided they had better move on. Because another brother had established a branch of the family business at Soldaia (in the Crimea of modern-day Russia), they went there. But when business on the farther side of the Black Sea proved poor, they moved eastward to an area near the Volga River (see map on page 35). Here they traded in jewels, salt, furs, wood, and probably slaves taken from the peoples of that area.

Continuing now in a northeasterly direction, the Polos journeyed to Bulgar. This was one of the centers of the Western Tartars—often called the Golden Horde because of their fondness for gold and because of the magnificence of their ruler's pavilion. Their lord was Birkai, one of the grandsons of the great Genghis Khan. Birkai, proving to be an unusually generous Mongol prince, gave the brothers such an abundance of goods in exchange for their jewels that they stayed an entire year in his domain.

As Nicolo and Maffeo were about to start for home fighting broke out between Birkai and his cousin Hulagu. Raiding parties and bandits made the road back to Constantinople dangerous for travelers, so the brothers decided to push eastward in the hope of finding a roundabout way home.

Loading their arabas—huge, two-wheeled carts drawn by horses, donkeys, or, in desert areas, camels—they set out. After journeying a month, much of that time in arid regions inhabited only by nomads, they reached the walled city of Bukhara, one of the crossroads of Central Asia. The city's tiled and blue-domed mosques and its bazaars crowded with Oriental wares and merchants were at first a welcome relief from travel. But soon the Polos found themselves completely marooned, for the road behind them had been blocked by warring parties, and the one leading eastward was also bristling with danger.

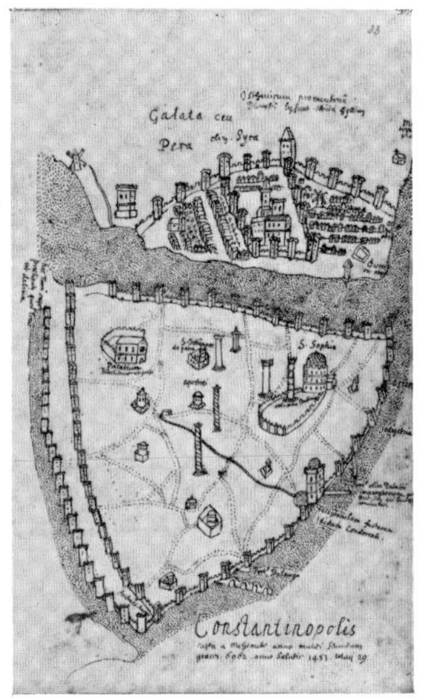

Constantinople stands on the European shore of the Bosporus, gateway to Asia. This 1453 map shows that the city is split by an inlet (called the Golden Horn): to the north is Galata, a commercial suburb; jutting into the Bosporus is the center of the city with its major buildings, including St. Sophia.

They languished a full three years in Bukhara, carrying on as much trade as possible, before a chance meeting freed them. An envoy of the Mongol lord Hulagu, returning from a mission in Persia, was introduced to them. The envoy was impressed by the strange ways of these "Latins" —as Europeans were known in Asia—and by their ability to speak the Mongol tongue. He invited them to accompany him to the court of the Great Khan Kublai in China, where, he assured the brothers, they would be received with honor. Welcoming the chance to leave Bukhara, to cross Asia under the protection of the Great Khan, and, not least, to open up a new market for their goods, the Polos accepted the invitation gladly.

All that is known of their long, arduous journey eastward comes from a few details that Marco Polo discloses in the introduction to the story of his own later travels. But it is certain that the mountains and deserts, the rivers and gorges they crossed remain to this day among the most rugged and perilous in the world. Even though the brothers traveled in the company of a high official, and were thus safe from interference, it took them a whole year to reach the Great Khan of the Mongols.

But it was worth the trouble, for the mighty Kublai welcomed them, and as his guests they were able to glimpse some of the wonders of his domain. The Polos were fortunate in this respect, for they were the first Europeans to visit China. A few missionaries had reached Mongolia but none had crossed into China. Why China remained so long closed to Western travelers makes a fascinating story.

As far back as the time of ancient Greece and Rome, products from China and India had gone by caravan to the markets of Europe. At the same time, some Western merchandise trickled into China, and in 327 B.C. the armies of

TEXT CONTINUED ON PAGE 38

TURKISH INFORMATION OFFICE

Two centuries after the Polos had passed through Constantinople on their way to Central Asia (see route below), St. Sophia was turned into a Moslem temple. Today, framed by four soaring minarets (above), the basilica is a Turkish museum that may be visited by Christians and Moslems alike.

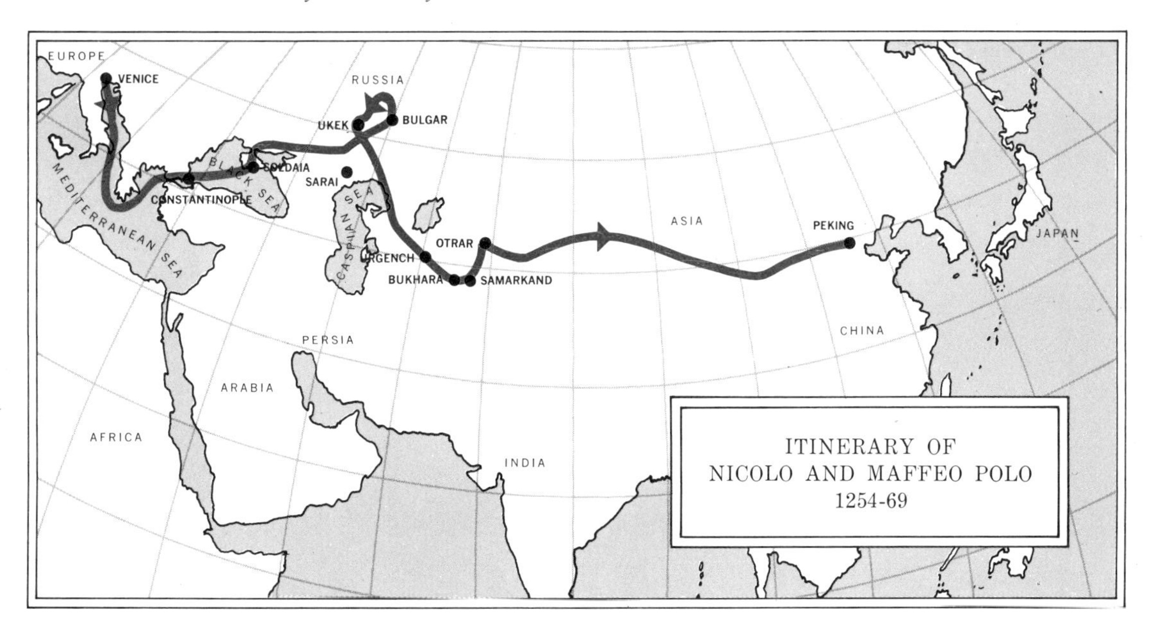

genetzer·
turci

Tooting horns and thumping on drums, a band of Turkish horsemen prance and plod their way through Palestine in the colored woodcut at left. The picture is from a 1486 book that records the events of a monk's journey to the Holy Land. The artist, named Reuwich, was one of the monk's traveling party.

TEXT CONTINUED FROM PAGE 34
Alexander the Great conquered Persia and even penetrated into India.

As early as the beginning of the empire of the Caesars, a stream of Oriental goods and wares, mainly silk but probably including cinnamon, rhubarb, iron, and furs, was flowing into Europe. At the peak of Roman luxury almost every well-to-do Roman owned silken garments. Critics of this extravagance complained of the self-indulgence of men who wore such garments and the shamelessness of women who exposed themselves in sheer silks. Despite their generous use of this material, there was so little knowledge of the place from which silk came that Romans long thought it grew on trees.

N.Y. PUBLIC LIBRARY, RARE BOOK DIVISION

A monk called William of Rubruck preceded the Polos into Asia. In this eighteenth-century engraving he appears before the draperied splendor of Batu Khan's pavilion.

As the Roman Empire declined in the third and fourth centuries and barbaric tribes made inroads from the north, trading became difficult. Romans were less and less able to afford luxuries from abroad. At the same time, the nomad tribes of Asia were harassing the caravan routes from China, and both Abyssinians and Arabs began to block the water routes through the Red Sea. The silk trade dwindled. Then in A.D. 542 two Christian monks from India smuggled the eggs of silk moths into Constantinople, and the silk trade with the East was doomed. Before long, the Byzantines had established enough of a silk industry to satisfy the shrinking needs of Europe. Gradually nomad Turks and Moslem Arabs, dominating Central Asia, cut off almost every contact between East and West.

The resulting interruption of trade and communication between the two halves of the known world was to last for nearly seven hundred years.

During that period, which was marked by widespread poverty and disorder, the West forgot what little it had known about the East. The Christian religion encouraged its followers to concentrate not on knowledge of the world, but on spiritual matters. Because learning was acquired from religious texts, students clung to ancient biblical notions of the earth. In the sixth century, for example, a scholarly monk, Cosmas, declared in a treatise on the universe that the world was a dome-shaped mountain rising in the midst of a vast ocean, with Jerusalem at the top.

While Europe groped through this twilight of backwardness and inertia, Chinese civilization, especially during the period of the T'ang dynasty (618–906), achieved new heights in education and the arts and also in industry, commerce, and invention. But the T'ang became weak and overrefined, and after a period of invasions and dis-

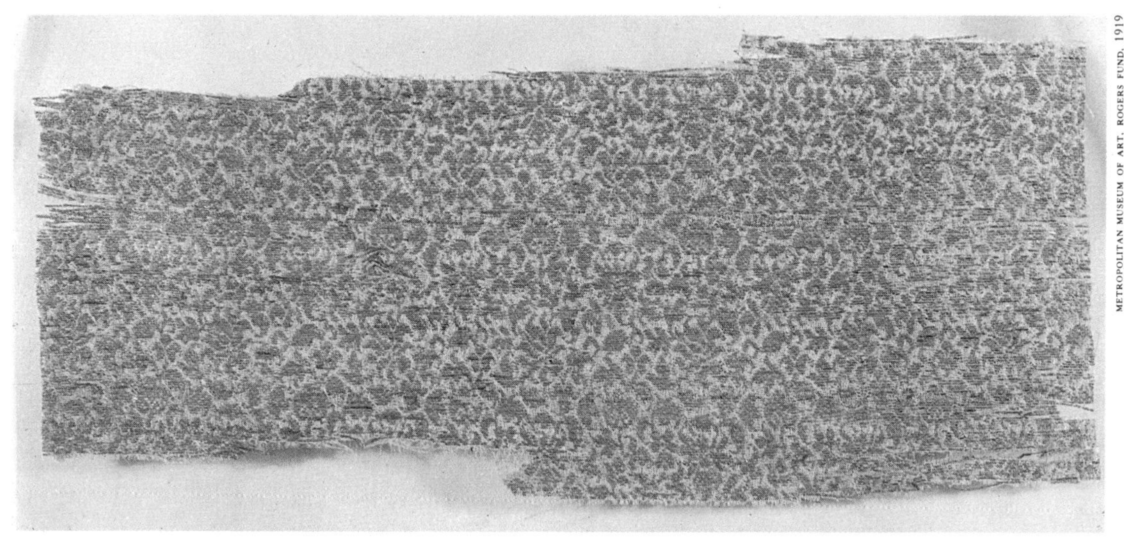

METROPOLITAN MUSEUM OF ART, ROGERS FUND, 1919

Soon after the Polos retraced the eastward trade routes, Chinese silk was seen again in Europe. Above is a piece of a silk garment worn by Pope Benedict XI. Below is the sleeve of a gold-leaf dalmatic, part of the vestments worn by a Church dignitary; it dates from the fourteenth century.

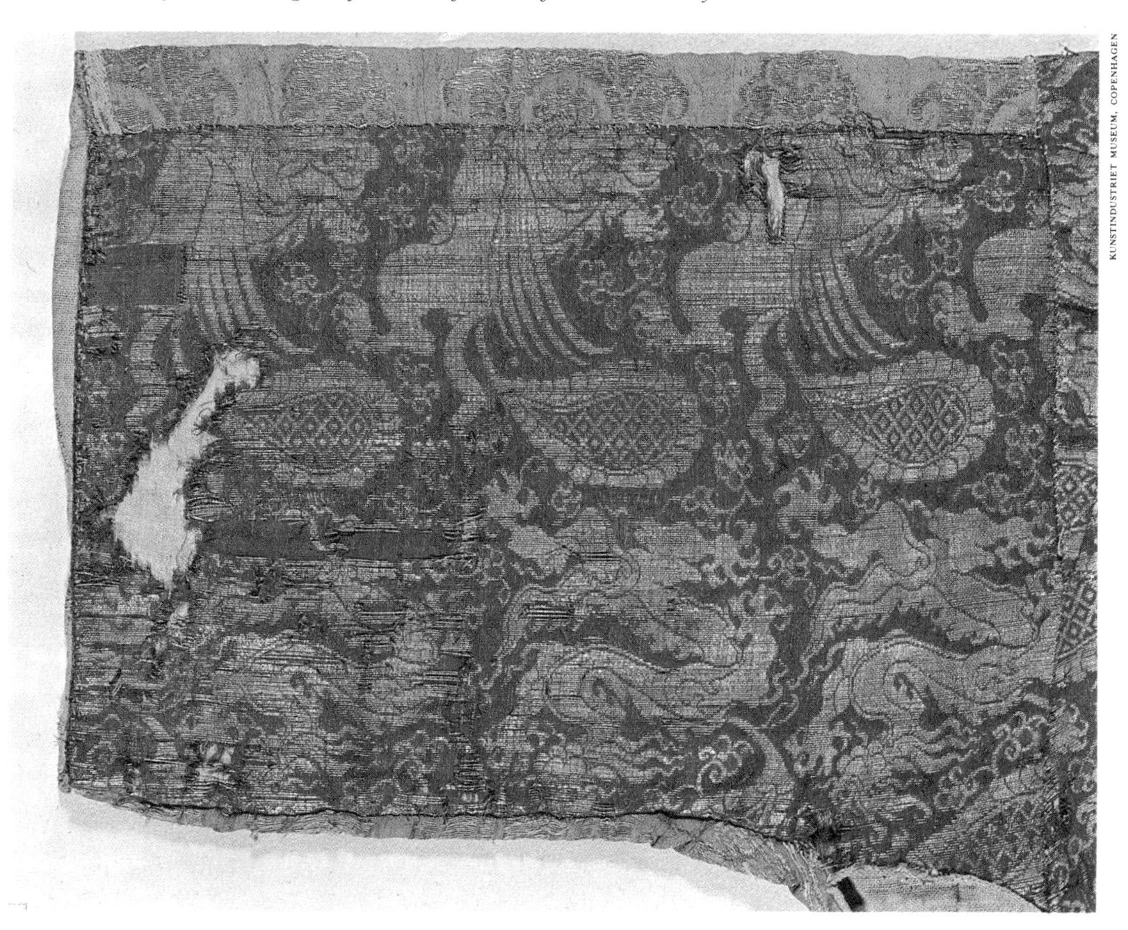

KUNSTINDUSTRIET MUSEUM, COPENHAGEN

COURTESY MUSEUM OF FINE ARTS, BOSTON

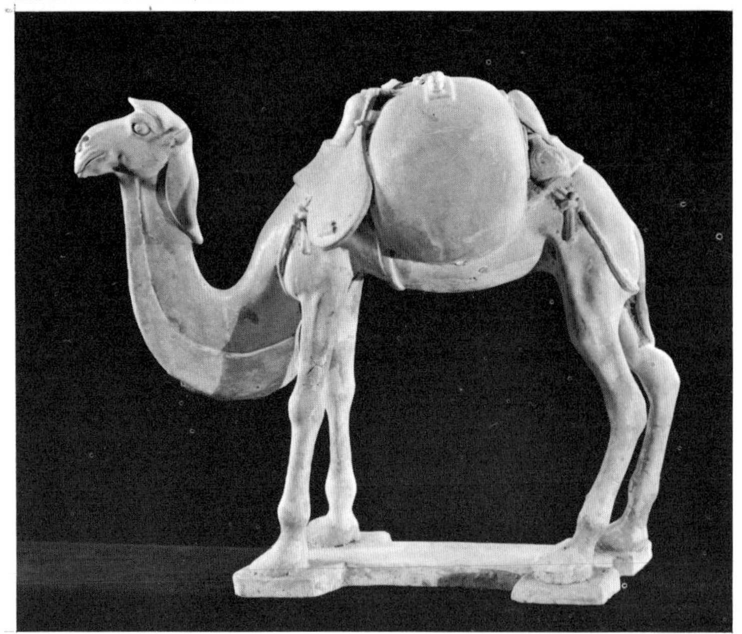

The Catalan Atlas, made in 1375, comprises eight wooden panels on which the known world appears. A detail from the atlas is at right, turned upside down to show a caravan which is supposed to represent Nicolo and Maffeo traveling by camel to Peking. At left is an exquisitely detailed pottery camel made in China at least three centuries before the Polos left home.

order, the Sung dynasty took over in 960. The Sung period lasted more than three hundred years and was a time of both practical and intellectual achievement. Firearms were invented; libraries grew; architecture developed into an art.

But over the years, the unfriendly tribes that threatened China's borders became more and more aggressive. Their hostility reached a climax early in the thirteenth century when the Mongol lord Genghis Khan united a great many of the nomadic Mongolian tribes and set out to conquer Asia (see dynastic chart on page 44).

Within the next fifty years, Genghis and the khans who succeeded him assembled one of the largest empires in history. By the middle of the thirteenth century, Mongol power had become so secure that the khans could afford to tolerate foreign visitors and even be hospitable to them.

The first traveler to cross Asia into the realm of the khans was a Franciscan monk, John of Plano Carpini, who was sent by the pope in 1245 to carry the Christian faith to the Mongol rulers and their hordes. It was a hopeless undertaking, but Friar John went through with it heroically. He reached the Mongol capital on the steppes just as a new great khan, Kuyuk, was being crowned. The monk spent four months in the Mongol camp, and though he did not win any converts, he carried back to Europe the first reliable description of Mongol civilization.

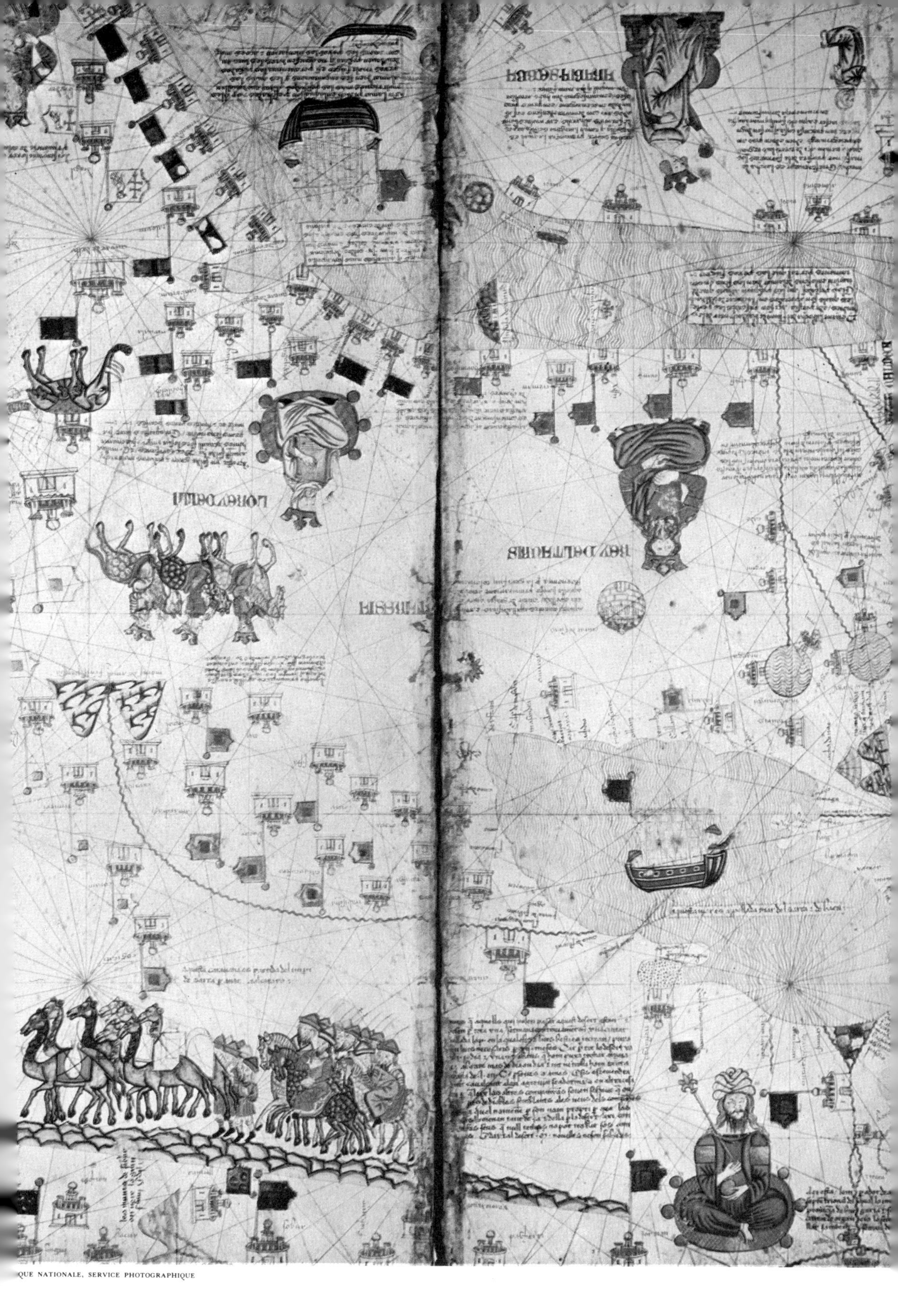

QUE NATIONALE, SERVICE PHOTOGRAPHIQUE

In 1252 another Franciscan, William of Rubruck, was sent east because of a rumor that Sartak, son of Batu Khan, had become a Christian. In his zeal Friar William managed to reach not only the territory ruled by Sartak near the Volga River, but even the throne of the Great Khan Mangu in far-off Mongolia. The monk's religious mission was a failure; Sartak proved not to be a Christian, and Friar William was unable to convert any Mongols. However, like his predecessor, he returned to Europe with an intimate and colorful account of Mongol life.

Unfortunately, little attention was paid to either of the friars; certainly the Polos were unaware of their travels. Nicolo and Maffeo were welcomed by Genghis' grandson Kublai, who had become Great Khan in 1260. He plied the Polos with questions about Europe's princes and governments and was particularly curious about the pope and Christian beliefs.

Pleased by the brothers' answers, Kublai gave them letters asking the pope to send one hundred of his most learned men—theologians who might be able to prove to Kublai the superiority of Christianity. He also gave the brothers a golden tablet that was supposed to guarantee their safe journey home. The tablet was inscribed with the words "By the strength of the eternal heaven, holy be the Khan's name. Let anyone who does not pay him reverence be killed." He also asked the Polos to return—and to bring with them some oil from the lamp above Christ's sepulcher in Jerusalem.

Little is known of the homeward expedition of the elder Polos other than the fact that it lasted three years. On reaching Acre, in northern Palestine, they learned that Pope Clement IV had just died. They told the story of their meeting with Kublai Khan to a papal representative, Theobald of Piacenza. Theobald advised them to wait until a new pope had been elected and then by all means to carry out their mission.

So in 1269, after fifteen years of traveling and trading in a thousand strange places across the whole breadth of Asia, the Polos came home. Only then did Nicolo learn that his wife had died long before. Whatever his grief, he must have been pleased to find his son Marco now a sturdy youth of fifteen.

The Polos' stay in the court of Kublai Khan is shown differently in two fourteenth-century French manuscripts. Above, they kneel like penitents before him. At right, attired as monks, they receive his golden tablet.

de son commandement.
Quant le seignour lor
ot en chargie tout sõ
message. Si lor fist
donner une table dor
en la quelle il estoit
contenu que les .iij. messages
en toutes les pars que il alas
sent leur deust estre donne, tou
tes leur mansions que besoig
leur fust et de chevaus & dom

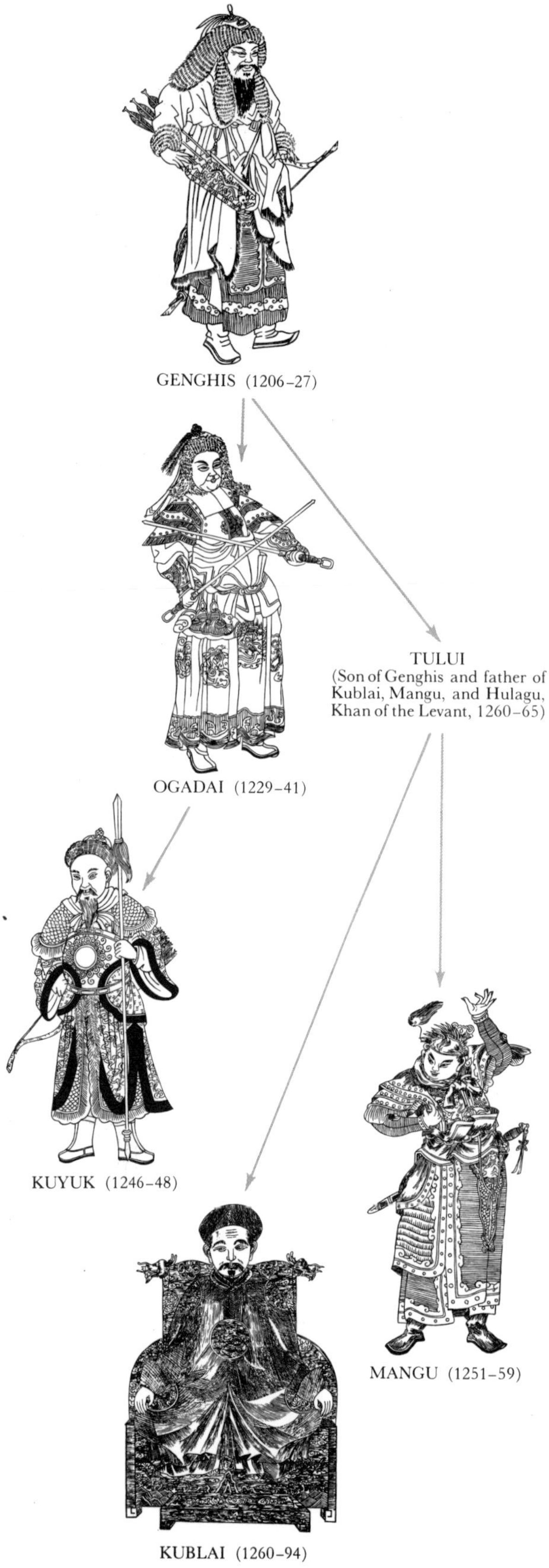

GENGHIS (1206–27)

OGADAI (1229–41)

TULUI
(Son of Genghis and father of Kublai, Mangu, and Hulagu, Khan of the Levant, 1260–65)

KUYUK (1246–48)

MANGU (1251–59)

KUBLAI (1260–94)

THE GREAT KHANS

At the head of the chart at left, which traces three generations of the house of Genghis Khan, is Genghis himself, holding a double-curved bow and a quiver of arrows. Under the rule of his son Ogadai, Genghis' kingdom in Central Asia became an empire extending first into parts of China, then to the very gates of Europe. After Ogadai died in 1241 (thirteen years before the Polo brothers set out for the East), the Great Khans Kuyuk and Mangu devoted themselves to the conquest and subjugation of China. It was Mangu's brother Kublai, another of Genghis' grandsons, who completed that brutal take over. Of all the Great Khans he was the most capable administrator, using Persians and other foreigners to help govern the Chinese—who were unimpressed by the Mongols' efforts to become Chinese in appearance and outlook. Kublai (seated at bottom) was the first Great Khan to abandon the warrior trappings of the Mongols. At right, in a copy of an ancient picture, Kublai wears the dragon-decorated robe of a Chinese emperor. When the Polos arrived to open a new chapter in the history of China, Kublai's power was strong enough for him to regard them not as a threat, but as an opportunity for contact with the West.

元世祖像

Nicolo, Maffeo, and Marco Polo's departure from Venice is seen in sequence in a miniature from a French manuscript of 1400. First the men are beside the Grand Canal. Then they board a tiny boat in the lagoon (top right). Finally, unfurling the sails of their galley (bottom), they head out to sea.

THE LONGEST JOURNEY

Nicolo and Maffeo Polo remained in Venice for two years, waiting for a new pope to be chosen. Nicolo even took a new wife, and his son Marco had a home for the first time in years. But the elder Polos had been wanderers too long and had seen too many of the wonders of the world to be content to settle down. Moreover, they had a mission to perform for the rich and powerful Kublai Khan.

Fearing that the Great Khan would think they had failed him, the Polos made plans to visit Palestine to fulfill the first of their promises to Kublai. And they decided to take young Marco with them.

Marco had listened to his elders' talk, which was salted with foreign phrases, and to their stories of the wonders and riches of China. Thus he was overjoyed when he learned he would accompany his father and uncle to the ends of the known earth, to all the far-off places he had heard them speak of. Knowing how long it had taken his father to reach China and return, Marco realized that he would be gone for a long, long time.

For years he had watched the ships come and go in the lagoons around Venice. There were swift, flat-bottomed fishing vessels with red and orange sails; seagoing galleys with proud sails and banks of rowers; ships of war with massive beaked prows for ramming an enemy—and huge engines called mangonels for hurling casks of "Greek fire." Now at last Marco would sail away in one of these ships.

Overnight the goods being unloaded on the quays acquired a special meaning for Marco. Here were cloves from the Moluccas, pepper and ginger from Malabar, cinnamon from Ceylon. On these wharves were varieties of resins and fragrant roots to make perfumes and incense and medicines—musk from Tibetan deer, myrrh from East Africa, frankincense from Arabia, and camphor from

Borneo. Here were diamonds from India, ivory from Zanzibar, sandalwood from Timor, scarves from Kashmir, muslin from Mosul, and Damascus steel for swords. Soon Marco would see with his own eyes the places from which all these things came.

After all the times he had stopped in front of shops to watch the craftsmen at work, it was a new experience to go with his father and uncle to buy the wares. Among the most fascinating artisans were the glassmakers, blowing gleaming bubbles into magical shapes. Elsewhere were goldsmiths and jewelers fashioning ornaments, and armorers making the weapons Crusaders would take to the Holy Land.

At last all was in readiness, and in the summer of 1271 the Polos set sail. As the seventeen-year-old Marco stood on the deck of the vessel and watched the spires and domes of Venice vanish behind him, he could hardly have dreamed he would be gone for twenty-four years and would see more of the world than any man up to his time.

Sailing down the Adriatic and out into the Mediterranean was an exciting beginning. Who knew what sudden storms or what attacks by pirates lay ahead of them. And who could tell what monsters might be lying in wait—for this was a time when voyagers believed the sea swarmed with creatures waiting to attack every vessel.

But the voyage was uneventful, and finally the Polos came in sight of the walls of Acre, the Palestinian stronghold that had been fortified by the Crusaders, and where for centuries pilgrims had stopped on their way to Jerusalem. Inside the town Marco gazed in wonder at the towers and palaces built by the Crusaders and at the nobles themselves, the pick of European chivalry, all arrayed in the richest attire.

After reviewing their commission from Kublai Khan with the legate Theobald, the Polos were given permission to go to Jerusalem to fetch oil from Christ's sepulcher, as Kublai had requested. Jerusalem had long been the holy city of Jews and Moslems as well as of Christians, and it had become as much a place of religious conflict as of pilgrimage. How that city's immense number of holy relics and shrines must have amazed young Marco.

The Polos were about to resume their journey when a messenger brought them good news: the legate Theobald himself had been chosen pope (he became Gregory X), and he wanted them to return to Acre at once. The new pope greeted them warmly and was eager to help them. But instead of a hundred learned men—as Kublai had re-

The majestically tall bell tower (left), the domes of St. Mark's Church (center), and the narrow gothic arches of the Doges' Palace are clearly visible in this 1486 woodcut of Venice. From the harbor, bustling with gondolas and barges, the Polos began their great expedition to the East.

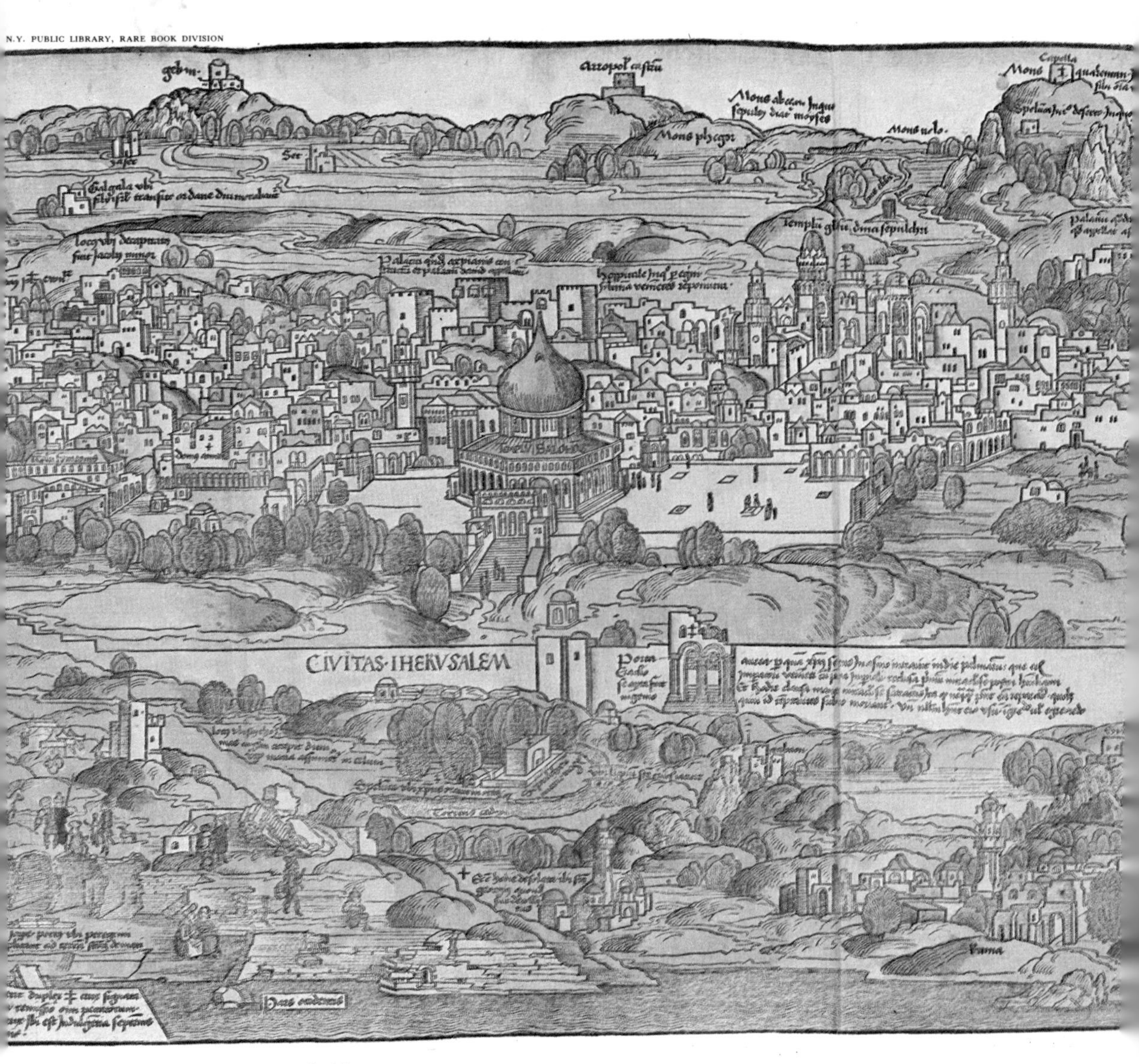

Jerusalem is in the center of this detail from a map of the Holy Land made in 1486. The Moslem Dome of the Rock is most prominent; to its right, in a cluster of towers, is the round, blue-topped dome of the Church of the Holy Sepulcher.

quested—all he could send with them were two scholarly Dominicans, Friar Nicholas of Vicenza and Friar William of Tripoli, and some gifts for the Great Khan.

They set out immediately. But no sooner were the travelers on the road than they learned that the Mamelukes, former slaves who now ruled Egypt, were laying waste and pillaging the countryside in front of them. Although the Polos carried the golden tablet of the lord of the Mongols as well as letters from the pope, the two monks were terrified. Along the road the travelers met a group of Knights Templars, who were pledged to give aid to pilgrims. The friars appealed for protection and were escorted back to the coast with the Templars. Despite the loss of these two important members of their party, the Polos pushed on.

In his book Marco Polo begins the story of his travels at Ayas, the eastern-Mediterranean city that was the usual jumping-off-place for travelers going eastward. Ayas had at least one familiar aspect: it was crowded with Venetian and Genoese traders. From there the Polos went through Lesser Armenia into a country called Turkomania (now Anatolia in eastern Turkey), which was famous for its fine carpets. The Turkomans were subjects of the far-off Great Khan, and one manuscript of Marco Polo's *Travels* tells how very tolerant the government of the Mongols was. As long as a man obeyed the laws, he could worship any god and in any religion he pleased. This must have amazed the Polos because European Christians were accustomed to making war on Saracens, persecuting Jews, detesting pagans, and scorning Greek Orthodox Christians.

The Polos' small caravan journeyed onward—sometimes attaching itself to a larger caravan. In this way, by stages, they moved into Greater Armenia, southeast of the Black Sea. Marco points out that this is the region of Mt. Ararat, where, according to the Bible and the local inhabitants, Noah's Ark had come to rest. Marco was also told that the mountain was covered with so much snow that it could not be climbed. Ararat is actually a very high mountain—almost 17,000 feet—and it is snow-covered, but it was finally climbed in 1829. The first climbers found no trace of Noah's Ark, but years later pieces of fossilized wood were discovered there. This discovery gave some people hope that the riddle of the ark had been solved, but no one has established precisely where the fossils came from.

BIBLIOTHEQUE NATIONALE, SERVICE PHOTOGRAPHIQUE

The caliph of Baghdad is led to prison in this miniature from a fourteenth-century French manuscript. The work, called Book of Marvels, concerns several medieval travelers, among them Marco.

Moving southeastward, Marco entered Zorzania (now part of Soviet Georgia). Here he reports seeing a geyser that gushed so much oil a host of camels was kept busy bearing it away. The oil, Marco informs his readers, was used to light lamps and as an ointment in treating rashes. This is an interesting example of how Europe in the Dark Ages had not only neglected the arts and learning of classical times, but had even forgotten useful discoveries. Oil, for example, had been used by the Egyptians, Romans, and Persians for lighting, heating, and even waterproofing. The Chinese, moreover, had learned to bore oil wells as early as 200 B.C., and using bronze drills and bamboo casings, had reached a depth of 3,500 feet.

Marco next makes the first of his many references to the Nestorian Christians scattered across Asia. This early branch of Christianity was named after Nestorius, a patriarch, or chief bishop, of Constantinople. He was deposed as a heretic in A.D. 431, and his followers went on to establish churches throughout the eastern half of the world. Although Nestorian doctrines were unacceptable to European Catholics, the Nestorians did carry the word of Christ clear across Asia. They founded a church in China in A.D. 638, nearly a thousand years before the Jesuit missionaries began to be seen there.

In his book Marco next describes Baghdad, the city of the caliphs, made famous by the tales from *The Arabian Nights* as the most romantic and mysterious city of the East. But Marco's description is so scanty that it is thought he did not visit the city himself. The most vivid story he tells of Baghdad concerns the capture of the city by Hulagu, Khan of the Levant, in 1258. Hulagu found that the caliph had amassed an immense hoard of gold but spent no money for soldiers to defend it. To teach the caliph a lesson, Marco says, Hulagu imprisoned him in a tower with all his treasure, told him to eat the gold if he could, and then let him starve to death. Others say the caliph was put to death in an even less pleasant way—by being wrapped in a robe and trampled by horses. Whatever the fate of the caliph, it

The first phase of Marco's journey, from his Venice home to the Turkish town of Erzurum, is traced on the map at right. Beyond Erzurum the Polos passed near Mt. Ararat a peak seventeen thousand feet high that is thought by some to be where Noah's Ark came to rest. The engraving below, made in 1686 places the ark atop a mountain at far left, high above the clouds.

N.Y. PUBLIC LIBRARY, RARE BOOK DIVISION

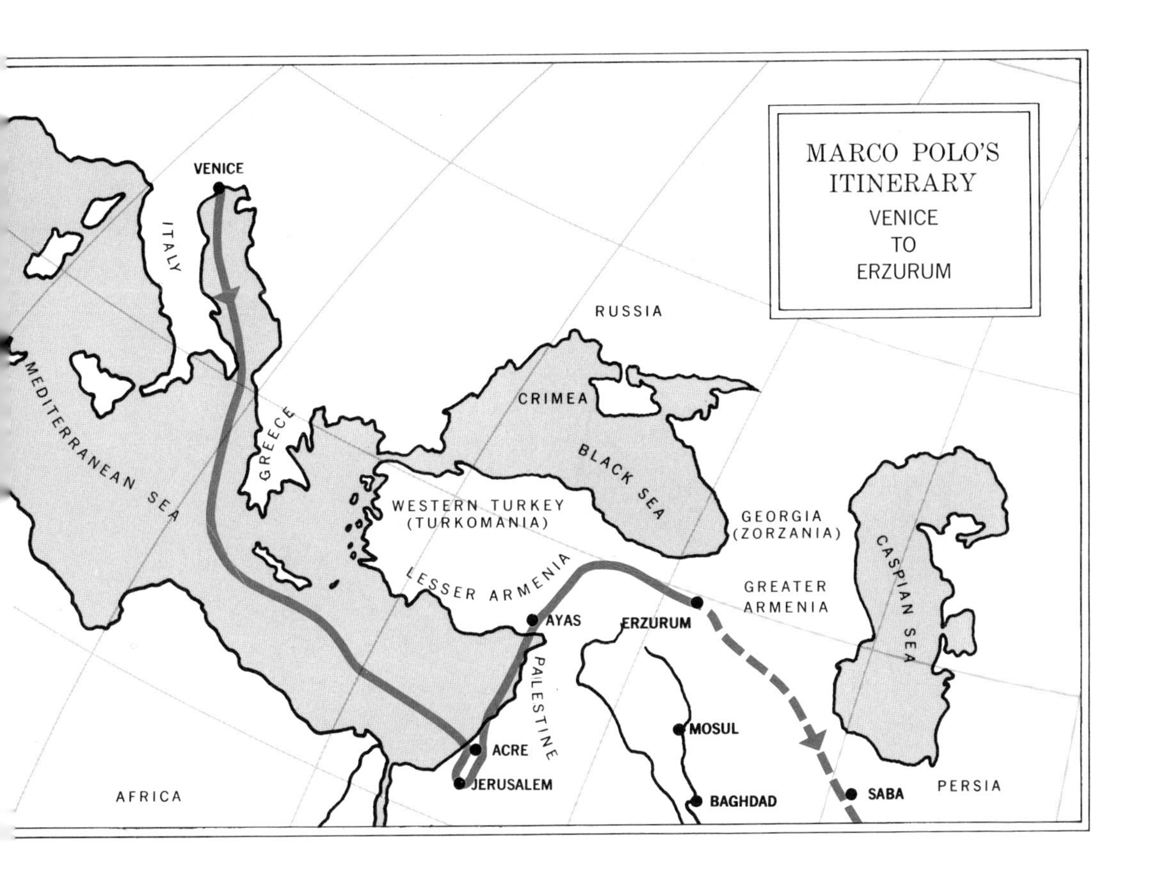

probably did not trouble Marco, since the ruler had been a Moslem, a hereditary enemy of Christians. In the very next chapter of his book Marco seems to reveal a prejudice when he says that most of the inhabitants of the rich city of Tabriz (in Iraq) are Moslems and are treacherous and wicked.

Traveling an average of about ten miles a day, the Polos came to the Persian town of Saba (just southwest of Tehran in modern Iran). This was said to be the city from whence the three Magi went to Bethlehem to adore the newborn Christ. Marco accepted this story when he was shown three bodies, said to be Balthasar, Gaspar, and Melchior, in a magnificent tomb, their beards and hair still intact. Here he also visited a sect of fire worshipers, probably followers of an ancient Persian religion founded by the teacher Zoroaster.

Marco explains the origin of this religion with the fanciful story that when the three Magi were leaving the infant Jesus, after presenting him with offerings of gold, myrrh, and frankincense, the infant gave them a box. On opening it during their journey home, they found in it a stone that

Although the Nestorian Christians were originally a Byzantine sect, they later emigrated to the East, and their outlook became more and more Oriental. The Nestorian religious painting at right, from a mural about Palm Sunday, shows a woman whose features are Chinese.

MUSEUM FÜR VÖLKERKUNDE, BERLIN

was supposed to signify they should remain as firm as stone in their faith. Not understanding the meaning of the stone, the Magi threw it away, whereupon it burst into flames. Marveling and repenting, they carried some of the fire home with them and thereafter adored it as a god and made sacrifices to it. It is hard to say whether Marco believed this explanation or thought it just a quaint tale.

Farther south was Kerman, known for its spurs, swords, and other arms made from fine steel, and for its needlework. The women of the city embroidered a variety of beautiful birds and beasts on curtains and coverlets. Leaving Kerman, the Polos climbed into the bitter cold of a mountain pass ten thousand feet high and then came down into a hot, well-populated plain. Here Marco describes a species of humped oxen (the zebu) and a kind of sheep with a tail so fat it sometimes weighed as much as thirty pounds.

Because he felt that the strange people and places he saw were more important than any adventures he himself had, Marco describes his personal experiences only on rare occasions. For instance, after entering an area made dangerous by a robber tribe known as the Caraunas, the Polos joined a large caravan. Soon the caravan was attacked; the ambush came in the midst of one of the dust "fogs" occurring in this region. Marco believed, as a result of tales he had heard, that the Caraunas could call up such fogs by means of diabolic incantations. Taken by surprise, the caravan was scattered in all directions. Although the Polos and part of their own little party escaped to a nearby village, the other members of the caravan were either murdered or sold into slavery. Marco, however, devotes only two sentences to this terrifying adventure and says nothing about what he must have felt and thought.

Having decided to go the rest of the way by sea, the travelers continued south toward the port of Hormuz on the Persian Gulf. Descending from the Plateau of Iran, they came to a country full of date palms and parrots. They found Hormuz crowded with traders offering spices, pearls, cloth of gold, elephant tusks, and other goods brought from India. So intense was the heat in summer that the inhabitants left the city and fled to the banks of a nearby river. Here, from nine in the morning until noon, when the sand-laden wind known as the simoom blew, the people immersed themselves in water up to their chins. As an example of the dreadful power of this wind, Marco was told of a large body of enemy soldiers who were caught by it as they marched against Hormuz. They were suffocated to the last

TEXT CONTINUED ON PAGE 58

OVERLEAF: *Hurling missiles with improvised siege weapons, Hulagu Khan assaulted the Moslem city of Baghdad in 1258, thirteen years before Marco's journey started. This miniature is from the Persian History of the World that was compiled in the fourteenth century.*

BIBLIOTHEQUE NATIONALE, SERVICE PHOTOGRAPHIQUE

TEXT CONTINUED FROM PAGE 55

man, and when the people of Hormuz went out to bury them, they found that the bodies had become brittle and crumbled to dust. This seemingly incredible effect of the simoom has been corroborated by later travelers.

When the Polos saw the vessels they would have to sail in, they lost all desire to complete their journey by sea. The boats, says Marco scornfully, each had only one mast, one sail, one rudder, and no deck. The wood in them was too hard for nails to penetrate, so the planks were held together by wooden pegs and then bound with a yarn made from the fiber of coconut husks. Hearing stories of the great storms on the Indian Ocean, the travelers were glad to return north to Kerman.

From there they moved northeastward along the Silk Route, once a highway not only for the silk traffic but for the spread of Buddhism and Nestorian Christianity. They

BIBLIOTHEQUE NATIONALE, SERVICE PHOTOGRAPHIQUE

The three Magi kings who carried gifts to the infant Jesus are thought to have belonged to a religious sect that revered fire; legend suggests they may have established the sect themselves. In a miniature from the French Book of Marvels (above), the Magi pay homage before an altar on which a fire burns. The picture at right shows the ruins of a Persian temple that was used by followers of the fire-worshiping religion of Zoroastrianism.

crossed a vast salt desert with only poisonous green waters on it, and, after more arid wastes, finally reached Tunocain. After the weeks spent in the desert, everything in Tunocain seemed very pleasant to the youthful Marco, and he declared that the women of this city were "the most beautiful in the world."

Marco may have been interested in the women of Tunocain, but he was fascinated by a fanatical Moslem sect, the Assassins, or *Hashishin*. The members of the sect were called by this name because allegedly they took hashish, a powerful drug. It was known that at the command of their grand master, the "Old Man of the Mountain" (actually an entire line of such leaders from 1090 to 1256), the Assassins had stabbed to death a shah of Persia, a grand vizier of Egypt, two caliphs of Baghdad, a few leading Crusaders, and other prominent men. Thus the

SPORT FILM, TEHRAN

Reclining comfortably with a bow and arrow close at hand, Hulagu Khan, Kublai's older brother, sips mare's milk in this Persian painting of 1575.

Assassins had made themselves the terror of Moslem Asia. The most widespread tale of their blind devotion was that of two young men who had climbed a high tower in the mountains near Damascus and then at a signal from their chief had plunged to their death.

It is easy to understand why Marco was eager to find out what inspired such incredible devotion. The explanation he heard was this: the original Old Man of the Mountain had built a fortified castle in the mountains of northern Persia, south of the Caspian Sea. Then, in a nearby valley, he had laid out the most lavish and enchanting gardens in the world, abounding in the finest fruit trees, flowers, fragrant shrubs, and sparkling streams. Set about the gardens were splendid pavilions, curiously wrought, ornamented with gold, and luxuriously furnished with paintings, silken hangings, and carpets. Into these pavilions were piped streams of wine, milk, honey, and pure water. And in each building were the loveliest maidens imaginable, matchless in dancing, singing, love making, and playing instruments.

The grand master had created this luxurious place so that he could reward those of his followers who most willingly committed the crimes, especially murder, that would spread his doctrine and his rule. He gathered the most vigorous and hot-blooded youths of the surrounding countryside and told them he had the power to transport them to the kind of paradise Mohammed had promised his followers. He then drugged several at a time with drinks of hashish and had them carried into the valley. When they awoke and began to enjoy the delights and marvels of the garden, they believed they were indeed in paradise. After a few days the men were drugged again and carried out of the garden and into the leader's castle. Recovering, they were of course disappointed to find themselves back on earth again. Then the chief promised to restore them to paradise if they carried out a murder for him—even at the risk of being killed in the act. In this way the chief recruited a band of men who went anywhere and happily committed any crime he desired. At the same time he acquired the reputation of possessing almost divine power.

For a century and a half the grand masters of this sect reigned with utmost tyranny, their crimes and power spreading as far as Syria and Egypt. Then the Mongols, led by Hulagu, drove into Persia. Hearing of the sect and its diabolical rule, the invaders besieged the Assassins' major stronghold. Only after three years, and the death of the reigning grand master, were the Mongols able to conquer the stronghold and demolish it.

The Assassins surely deserved their reputation as murderous fanatics. But it is doubtful that their fanaticism was the result of taking hashish or the lure of "gardens of paradise." The truth seems to be that they had supreme faith in their leaders' powers and promises and were thoroughly trained to believe that obedience and sacrifice would bring them a heavenly reward.

From Tunocain the Polos made their way to Balkh, in northern Afghanistan, where trade routes between East and West converged. Once a splendid city with many palatial dwellings, Balkh had been assaulted by Genghis Khan in 1222, and much of it was still in ruins. Beyond the city, the travelers moved for more than a hundred miles through a plain from which the inhabitants had been driven into mountain strongholds by invaders.

Another twelve days brought them to a range of mountains that yielded a pure white salt so precious that people came from as far away as thirty days' journey to get it. Beyond these mountains was the province of Badakhshan, noted for mines that produced rubies as well as sapphires

The Polos planned to proceed by sea from Hormuz, but they changed their minds when they saw how unseaworthy and crowded the available ships were. Here the travelers try to board a vessel that is already weighed down by a camel, a horse, and a small, gift-laden elephant.

Glazed earthenware bowls were a popular art form in Persia when the Polos were there. At the center of this bowl, a woman is strumming a lute. Along the rim are smaller images of her in other attitudes.

BODLEIAN LIBRARY, OXFORD

and lapis lazuli. The shrewd king of this province limited the mining of the rubies so as to maintain their rarity and their value.

Here once again is a fleeting glimpse of what Marco himself experienced during the journey. After explaining how the climate in the mountains of this province was known to cure fevers, he—or rather the scribe who took down his narrative—says: "Having been confined by sickness in this country for nearly a year, he [Marco] was advised to seek a change of air by going into the mountains. There he soon got well." Thus in a casual sentence or two Marco accounts for an entire year of his journey.

After his recovery, the Polos entered the Vale of Kashmir. Marco confirmed its reputation for being inhabited by sorcerers—masters of the black arts and devilish enchantments. Later he was to see these men performing their magic at the court of Kublai Khan.

A passage in Marco's book describes an Asian religious sect whose chief was called the Old Man of the Mountain. He lived in "a beautiful valley enclosed between two lofty mountains [where] he had built a luxurious garden, stored with every delicious fruit and fragrant shrub that could be procured." In this garden were "dainty and beautiful damsels, accomplished in the arts of singing [and] playing upon all sorts of musical instruments . . ." (right). The Old Man himself is pictured at left, outside the "strong and impregnable castle" that stood at the entrance to his vast earthly paradise.

Continuing northeastward, the travelers ascended the lofty Pamirs where three mighty mountain ranges meet, and which the natives call the Roof of the World. Among the wild animals Marco saw there were very large sheep with curling horns, each horn as much as four and one-half feet long. Although William of Rubruck, one of the monks who preceded Marco, had already described this creature, it is now known, in Marco's honor, as *Ovis poli.* The mountains in this area were so high (some peaks rising to 19,000 feet) that there were no birds near the summit. The air, as Marco keenly observes, was so rare that fires gave less heat and did not cook food as well as they did farther down.

Descending into Kashgar, with its fine gardens, orchards, and vineyards, the travelers found themselves at last on the fringes of China.

The caravan route they followed was the southern

BIBLIOTHEQUE NATIONALE, SERVICE PHOTOGRAPHIQUE

branch of the Silk Route. It led them to the ancient city of Khotan, where they saw men digging pieces of jade out of the dry river beds—as they do even now. The precious stone was found in colors ranging from white and yellow to dark green, vermilion, and even black. It was taken by caravan to China to be carved and polished into many kinds of beautiful objects.

Passing through increasingly arid regions, the travelers came to one of the world's great deserts, the Takla Makan (in present-day Sinkiang province), which stretches for hundreds of miles to the east. At the edge of the desert they rested and prepared to cross it, facing the possibility that if they ran out of food they might have to eat some of their beasts.

There were twenty resting places on the desert. But the water at many of these was not enough for a caravan of more than fifty persons, and in two or three places it was brackish and bitter. The travelers saw not a bird or beast anywhere, but only from time to time the bleached bones of men or animals. Moreover, many frightening stories were told of the eerie things heard and seen in the desert. All these, it was commonly believed, were the work of evil spirits. If a man fell behind his caravan and lost sight of it, he would begin to hear voices or the noise of caravans, and he would become confused and go astray. Or he would see figures that looked like his traveling companions, and following them, he would be lured to his death.

Sometimes travelers would hear musical instruments, singing, drums, or the clash of arms. All the things that Marco mentions have since been reported by other travelers and have been explained scientifically: the sounds are caused by the shifting of sands or the falling of sand cliffs among the dunes. Areas of this kind are in fact often given such names as "singing sands." As for the visions, they are mirages caused by heat waves, and they are completely bewildering to someone who is lost and beset by thirst.

A month later they came out of the desert and into the city of Shachow (now called Tunhuang). Marco found that the people here worshiped idols and made sacrifices to them. The burial ceremonies—apparently Buddhist—seemed very peculiar to the Venetian youth. For instance,

METROPOLITAN MUSEUM OF ART, GIFT OF HORACE HAVEMEYER, 1941

A sultan is surrounded by his submissive court in the Persian bowl-painting above, made in 1210. At left, from the Persian History of the World, Hulagu's men are ransacking the fortress of the Old Man of the Mountain.

if the astrologers who guided the people told them to preserve a dead body until a more favorable date for disposal, it was embalmed, sealed in a casket, and kept for as long as six months. Each day during this time food for the dead man was set next to the casket. When the prescribed day arrived, the people burned the body along with paper figures of servants, cattle, and all the things they thought the man would need in the next world.

Because the next two districts that Marco describes were far off his route, he probably did not visit them at this time. He says that one of them, Chinghintalas, produced a remarkable substance that did not burn when thrust into a fire. From a traveling companion, "a very intelligent Turkoman," Marco learned that the substance was mined, dried, pounded clean, spun into thread, and woven into cloth. Obviously, the substance that Marco describes was asbestos.

The next large city to which the Polos came was Kanchow; here trading proved so satisfactory that they remained for a full year. Then the travelers moved through the kingdom of Tangut (probably in Kansu province of

From Erzurum, the Polos crossed nearly five thousand miles of mountains, deserts, and prairies until they were finally led to Kublai Khan's summer palace at Shangtu.

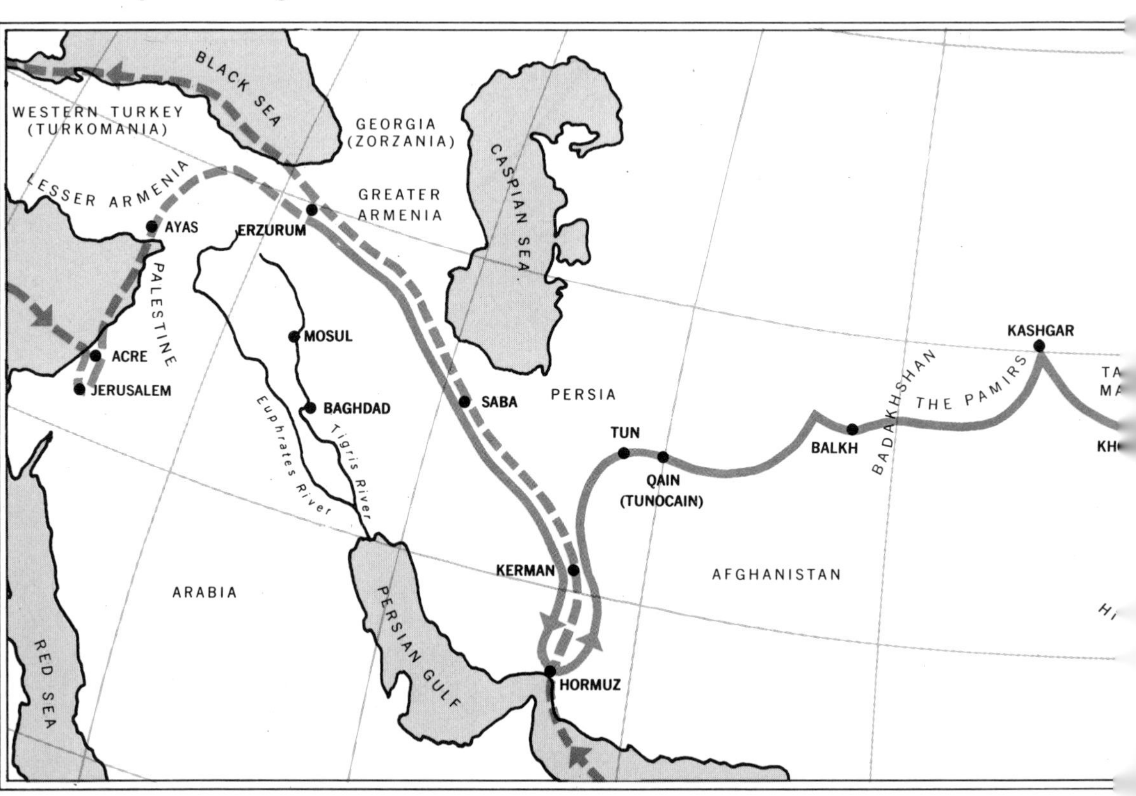

modern China) and came among people who were plainly Oriental—men with small noses, black hair, and nearly beardless faces. Here Marco was much interested by the animals known as yaks; he thought their wool so fine that he later took some of it back to Venice. He also tells how the finest musk in the world, a main source of European perfumes, was taken from a gland of a tiny antelope of this region.

Along with the accurate and reliable reports on things he saw himself, Marco occasionally includes a story with little basis in fact. At one point he repeats the tale that Ung Khan, who had been a Mongol chieftain in the province through which Marco was passing, was the legendary Prester (*priest* or *presbyter*) John. Prester John was said to have been a Christian who became ruler of a great empire located somewhere in Asia or, according to later and erroneous accounts, Ethiopia. Aside from the fact that Ung Khan was probably a Nestorian Christian, the story of Prester John was mostly the result of rumor and exaggeration.

When the Polos were still about forty days' journey

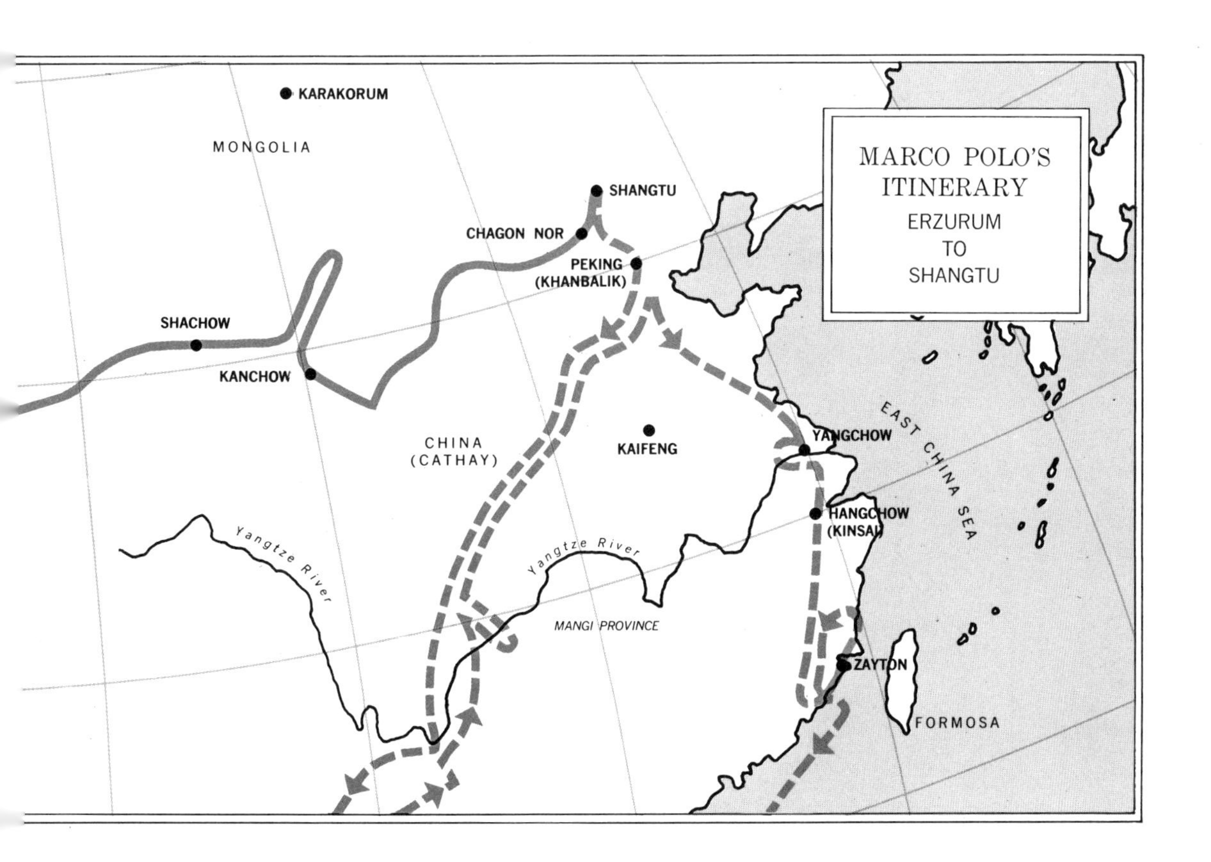

GOVERNMENT OF INDIA TOURIST OFFICE

from their destination, they were met by an escort from the Great Khan and led to his magnificent summer residence in Shangtu, north of Peking. So they made the last lap of their great journey in royal style.

Upon their arrival they were received most graciously by Great Khan Kublai and his court. The travelers prostrated themselves before him, bending their heads to the ground in the customary kowtow (literally "knock-head"). Following a lavish banquet, Nicolo and Maffeo were asked to report on their travels and particularly their negotiations with the pope. Kublai listened most attentively to their account and thanked them for the sacred oil they had brought from Jerusalem.

Noticing young Marco, Kublai asked who he was, and Nicolo answered, "This is my son and your servant." Thereupon the Great Khan replied, "He is welcome and it pleases me much." Then he ordered Marco to be given a place among his highest courtiers and arranged for a celebration in honor of the Polos' return.

On their way to the realm of Kublai Khan, the Polos journeyed around, not over, the towering Himalayas (left). In a miniature from the fourteenth-century Book of Marvels (above), the elder Polos kneel like monks before the mighty Kublai, who has been made to seem a benign and gentle patriarch.

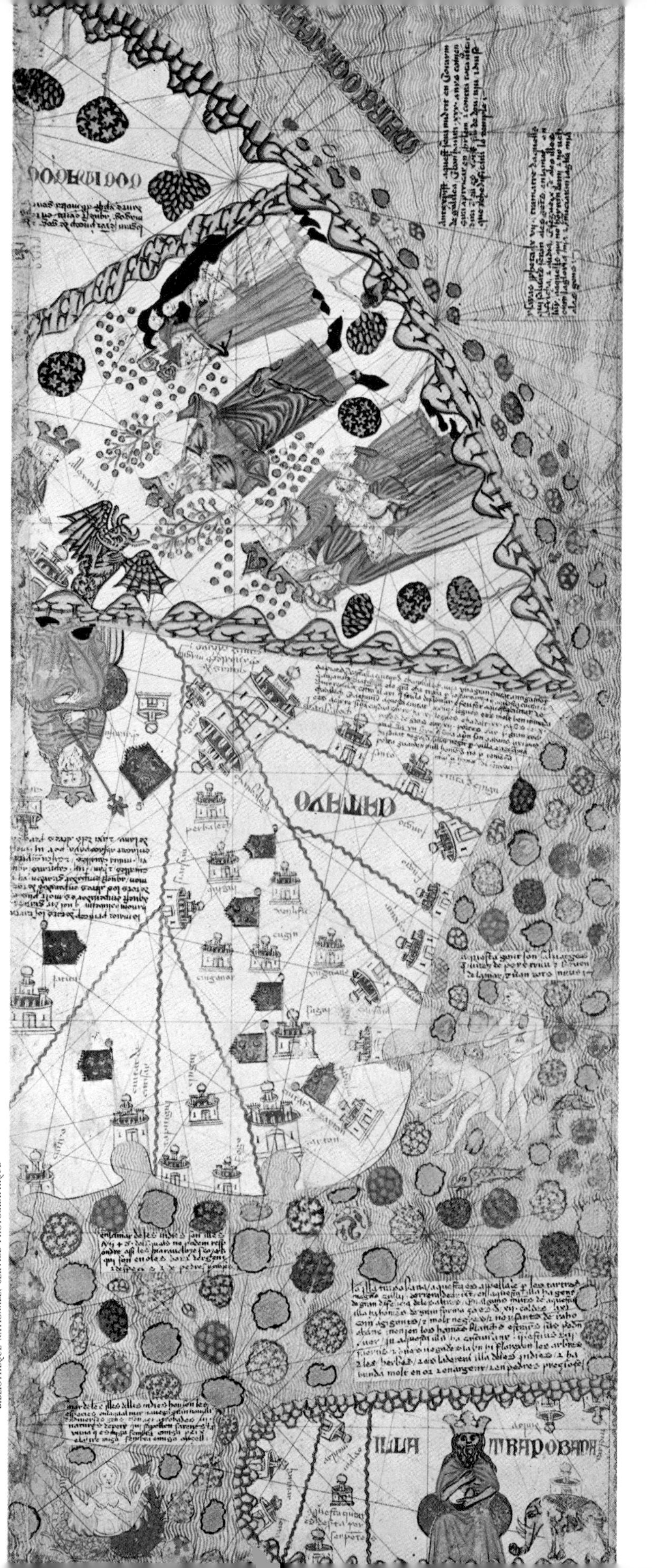

BIBLIOTHEQUE NATIONALE, SERVICE PHOTOGRAFHIQUE

AMERICAN MUSEUM OF NATURAL HISTORY

CHINA'S MYSTERIOUS GREAT WALL

To keep the barbarians out and the Chinese in, the Great Wall of China was built some 1,500 years before Marco Polo's caravan penetrated the borders of Kublai Khan's empire. Climbing over mountainous ridges and plunging into chasms, twisting, turning, and halting before finding its way across northern China, it is the largest stone construction ever made by man. Along most of its 2,000-mile total length, six horsemen could ride abreast. The wall is indeed a massive monument to the single-mindedness of the emperor who ordered it to be built, and to the backs and hands of the one million laborers who died in its construction. Despite deterioration over the centuries, parts of the Great Wall stood in Marco's time (and stand today—below). Yet, strangely, he never mentions seeing it on his way from barbarian territory into China (which he calls Cathay). At left is a section of one of the most famous world maps based on Marco's travels, the Catalan Atlas of 1375. This section shows all of China, including Kublai's Grand Canal (running vertically at center), but no trace of the Great Wall.

V

THE MONGOLS

Early in their journey eastward the Polos had met bands of Mongols with their flocks and herds and huge tents. From their previous travels Nicolo and Maffeo were thoroughly familiar with such people, but for Marco it was a fresh and exciting experience. Knowing that Kublai Khan was a Mongol and that it was the Mongols who had threatened to overrun parts of Europe a few decades earlier, Marco observed them curiously. He mingled with them whenever he could, so that by the time he reached the court of the Great Khan he had some understanding of their language. He also learned much about the sudden and dramatic rise to power of the Great Khan under whose protection he and his elders were traveling.

COLLECTION OF NATIONAL PALACE MUSEUM, CHINA

When the Polos arrived in Shangtu in the spring of 1275, the Mongol empire was at its height, extending from the Pacific Ocean to the kingdom of Poland. And yet the empire was scarcely three generations old. Less than eighty years before, the Mongols (or Tartars, as they were known in Europe) had been only scattered tribes of horse-mounted nomads roaming the high prairies, or steppes, southeast of Lake Baikal.

For many centuries these men with the short, bowed legs, longish bodies, broad, almost hairless faces, flat noses, high cheekbones, and eyes narrowed by cold winds and glaring sun had wandered the plains of Mongolia with their flocks and herds. When not hunting or making war they moved quietly from grazing land to grazing land. Only during the brief spring was their homeland, the boundless steppes, congenial. For the rest of the year the land was unsparing—scorching and dry in summer and lashed by icy winds in winter. From it the nomads doubtless acquired

These portraits of Genghis Khan (above) and his successor, Ogadai (right), are taken from a copy of a thirteenth-century Chinese album of emperors.

TAN MUSEUM OF ART, GIFT OF MRS. EDWARD S. HARKNESS, 1947

their hardiness and endurance, and their disregard for the value of human life.

A Mongol horde (from the Turkish word *ordu*, meaning a nomad camp or troop) lived in huge, beehive-shaped tents made of gray or black felt whitened with chalk and stretched over a latticelike framework. When the horde moved on, it usually mounted most of these tents, called *yurts*, on carts that according to Friar William of Rubruck were as much as twenty feet wide between the wheels and were drawn by as many as twenty-two bullocks. The driver stood in the door of the *yurt* as he drove. When the tent was set down, the floor was spread with beaten cow dung sprinkled with sand and occasionally covered with a rug. The fire was fed—as it still is on the nearly woodless steppes—with chunks or pressed bricks of dried dung, and the smoke passed through a neck-shaped opening at the top.

Since the nomads did no farming and could expect to find only a few wild vegetables, they relied chiefly on meat and milk for food. Some had large flocks of sheep, goats, and oxen, but most nomads ate whatever they could catch, including dogs and rats, and finished an animal down to the blood and intestines. In their saddlebags they always carried strips of dried meat—generally horseflesh—and cakes of dried milk. But the drink they enjoyed most of all was kumiss, fermented mare's milk, which had a slowly intoxicating effect.

In cold weather a Mongol man traditionally wore a fur

With one hand at his belt, another clutching a weapon, Genghis Khan stands before his tent in the miniature at left. The picture, from the History of the World, reflects a Persian concept of the elegance and splendor of a Mongol ruler's encampment. At right, two Mongols groom their horses in this copy of a painting by Chao Meng-fu, the most famous artist of the Mongol period.

MUSEE GUIMET, PARIS

cap, a sheepskin coat with one layer of wool next to the body and one layer outside, and riding boots with thick felt socks pulled over them. In war he donned a leather helmet banded with iron and equipped with a leather neck-guard, and sometimes he used layers of cowhide to protect himself and his horse. A Mongol warrior carried a wicker shield, several bows, a quiver of arrows, a file to sharpen arrowheads, and a battle-axe. Often he also carried a lance with a hook below the point—useful in dragging an enemy from his horse. On a long ride in wintry weather a Mongol would wrap his pony's legs in yak hides and warm himself by opening a vein in the animal's leg, drinking the blood, and then closing the wound. He could ride two days and nights without dismounting, sometimes sleeping in the saddle while his horse grazed. And he could cross a river by roping ponies together and clinging to them as they swam. Mongol ponies could get along without hay or grain, being able to paw through snow to reach grass or through earth to get at roots.

Long before Marco passed among the Mongols, they had begun to acquire slaves who assisted in the daily life of the horde. Nevertheless, a Mongol woman was spared none of the household drudgery. She cut fresh meat into strips and dried it so thoroughly that it could be stored for years. She fashioned oxhide into bags and stitched horsehide into sandals and boots. She churned butter, and then by boiling it and stuffing it into sheep's paunches, kept it from ever going rancid. She soured buttermilk left over from the churning, boiled it till it curdled, and dried the curds to an iron hardness; then in winter she poured hot water over the curds and produced a tart drink, a luxury in an area where the water might be foul. She made felt by beating wet sheep's wool into tangled fibers, pressing it into strips, and letting grazing ponies drag it about to give it a finish. When tending the herds she sat astride her horse and wore breeches and boots like a man. If need be she could shoot a wolf or accompany her man to war. She never washed her garments, for that would offend the spirits of the streams, and on the rare occasions when she washed herself, she did so by taking a mouthful of water from a vessel and spurting it into her hands.

It was common for a man to take more than one wife and also for the sons of a dead man to marry his widows. In time of war a woman could be carried off in a raid, become the property of one of the raiders, and bear his children until she was redeemed from captivity. So the first

In a seventeenth-century Persian drawing a heavy, unwieldy load is lifted onto a camel's back. In the course of his travels, Marco used many of these obliging beasts.

wife of Genghis Khan was stolen but was redeemed, bringing back a baby who was later accepted as Genghis' eldest son.

The Mongols had only a primitive kind of religion. It recognized a supreme being, the god of the sky, but he played little part in their lives. They were superstitious, believing that sickness was caused by evil spirits that could be driven out only by a *shaman*, a kind of medicine man, and their fortunes were read from the cracks that appeared in the shoulder-blade bones of a sheep when the bones were thrust into a fire.

Occasionally around a campfire at night the nomads danced to the music of crudely made drums, fiddles, and guitars and to the clapping of hands. But their favorite pastime when not hunting or fighting was lying in their tents drinking kumiss. Ruthless in war, they were nonetheless friendly and hospitable in time of peace.

One of the most important events in Mongol history occurred probably in 1162, for it was then that a child was born to the chieftain of a small Mongol tribe. Hounded and shortly afterward killed by his enemies, the father never dreamed that his son, called Temuchin, would one day become the first ruler of a vast Mongol empire. Undaunted by his father's enemies, Temuchin had become known for his daring and aggressiveness by the time he was seventeen. He led his clan on so many fierce raids that tribe after tribe either was conquered or absorbed without a fight. In time Temuchin organized the nomads into an army, with tribes converted into regiments. War and the chase, he believed, were the only fitting activities for a man, and he taught his men iron discipline, endurance, mobility, and love of conquest.

"The greatest joy a man can know," he declared, "is to conquer his enemies and drive them before him; to ride their horses and take away their possessions; to see the faces of those who were dear to them wet with tears; and to clasp their wives and daughters in his arms."

METROPOLITAN MUSEUM OF ART, GIFT OF A. W. BAHR, 1947

The Mongols frequently put on circuses to show off their remarkable horsemanship skills. This picture, a copy of a handscroll painted in China by

In 1206, when Temuchin was forty-four, chieftains from far and wide came together amid a sea of tents in Karakorum on the Mongolian steppe, and prostrating themselves before him, proclaimed him Genghis Khan, meaning roughly "Universal Lord." After that, Genghis haughtily refused to pay tribute to the powerful empire of the Chin, or Kin, as the rulers of northern China were known. When a Chin envoy came to him demanding that he pay tribute and also kowtow to the south, Genghis obediently faced south—and spat. War followed, and the Chin held out stubbornly. After more than twenty years of continual fighting, only a part of their empire was conquered, including the Chin city of Yenching (modern Peking).

Then the members of a peaceful Mongol mission sent to the Moslem ruler of Khwarizm in Persia were murdered. Swearing vengeance, Genghis Khan assembled 129,000 men and 390,000 horses and surged westward across Central Asia, burning and plundering as he went. Always before assaulting a city he gave the enemy's bravest men a chance to join him. Then he struck, enslaving some but

TEXT CONTINUED ON PAGE 84

the great Chao Meng-fu, shows the climax of such an event. Each rider is demonstrating his most spectacular feat of horsebackriding ability.

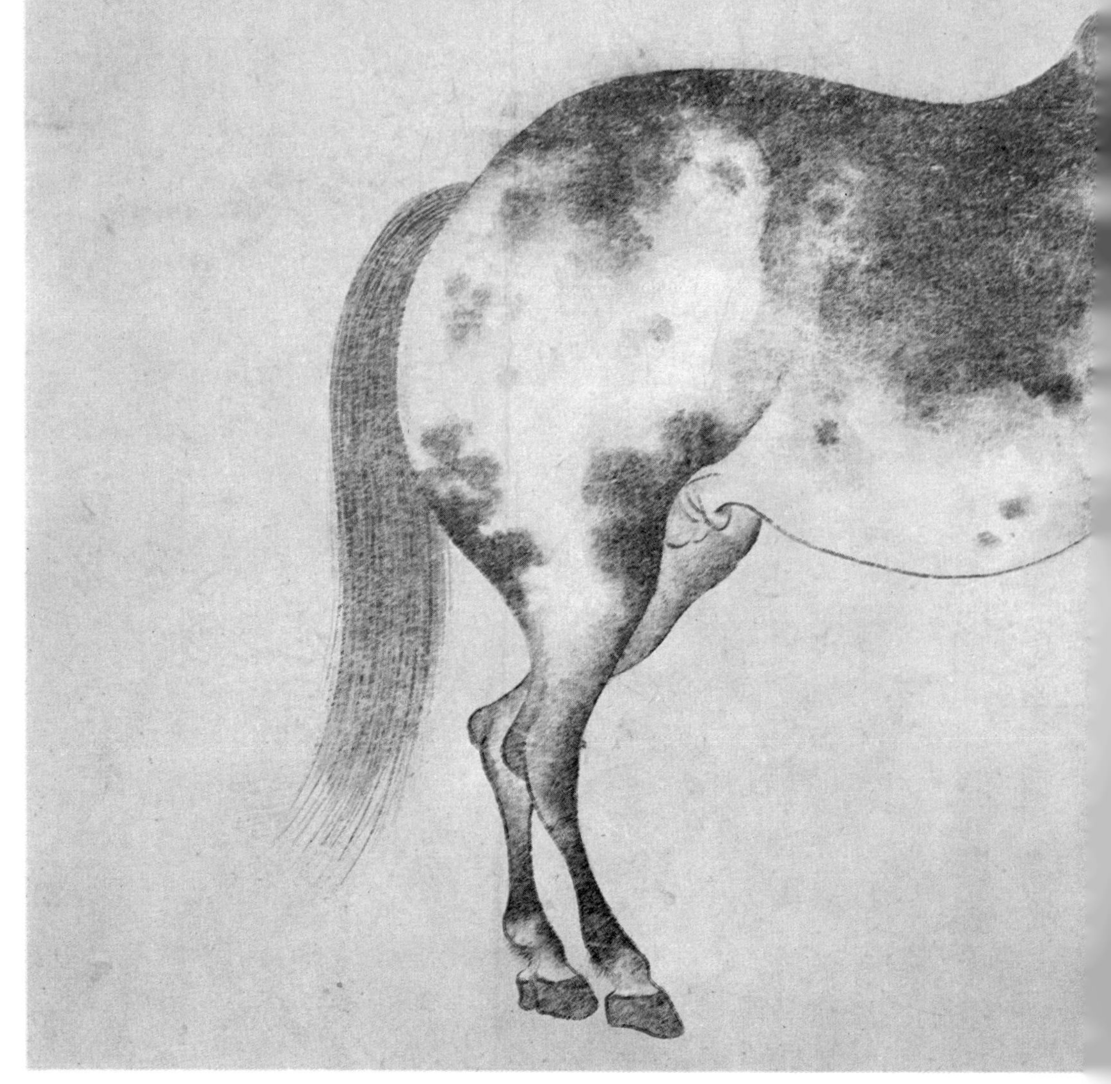

Mongol pride in horseflesh is expressed in this drawing made in 1347. The artist, who may have writt

COURTESY OF THE SMITHSONIAN INSTITUTION, FREER GALLERY OF ART, WASHINGTON, D.C.

ı at upper left, showed a horse both more noble and more intelligent looking than the floppy-hatted groom.

TEXT CONTINUED FROM PAGE 81

slaying most, and leaving behind a heap of smoking ruins. More than once Genghis Khan obliterated a particularly stubborn city—such as Urgench, east of the Caspian Sea—to the point where a few years later horses could graze on its site.

In 1225 he returned to Mongolia, leaving his greatest general, Subotai, to make a reconnaissance through Georgia and into Russia as far as the Volga River. Like his master, Subotai left a wake of death and destruction, and he gave rise to the first rumors to reach Europe of the terror that was surging out of the East. Finally Subotai withdrew.

One Eastern chronicler estimated that by the time of his death in 1227, Genghis Khan and his hordes had done to death millions of people in northern China alone. Tales of Mongol cruelty quickly spread throughout Asia. One story tells of a lone Mongol who rode into a village and killed all the men in it, not one daring to resist. Another account tells that after the capture of Urgench, each of the fifty thousand Mongol invaders slew twenty-four inhabit-

Upon the death of Genghis Khan in 1227, Mongol rule passed to his son Ogadai. In the miniature at left, the grieving Mongols gather around the bier containing Genghis' body. At right, the new Great Khan, Ogadai, is seated on a golden throne. One of his brothers kneels and swears allegiance.

ants. Then the Mongols destroyed a dam above the city and let the Amu Darya River wash all traces of life from the ruins.

Warriors willing to join their conquerors, and craftsmen and others able to serve the khans, escaped systematic extermination by the Mongol hordes. In fact, Genghis prohibited any warfare or feuding after he had conquered an area, and thus he gradually established peace in all of Moslem Asia. It was so peaceful, one writer said with a touch of flattering exaggeration, that "a damsel with a nugget of gold on her head could wander safely throughout the realm."

Genghis was succeeded by one of his four sons, Ogadai, a good-natured, openhanded man who loved eating and drinking and had no less than sixty wives. He sought to carry on the work of conquest where his father had left off.

First he had Subotai launch a campaign against the southern territory of the Chin empire. Subotai crossed the Great Wall of China, which had long since become a

SOVFOTO

Genghis Khan's greatest warrior, a general named Subotai, appears in all his fighting regalia in the drawing above. It was he who led the Great Khan's army into southern Russia. At left the Mongols attack Russian troops who resist vainly from behind their palisade.

highway for invaders rather than a barrier to them. To conquer the walled city of K'aifeng he ringed it with another wall many miles around and starved the city into submission. But Ogadai's chief adviser, Ye-Lü Ch'u-ts'ai, a wise and learned man, persuaded Ogadai not to slay the million inhabitants of the city. He pointed out that if they were spared, they could then continue to pay taxes and make beautiful things for Ogadai.

At K'aifeng, too, the Mongols faced the *huo-p'ao*, the frightening weapon in which sulphur and saltpeter (gunpowder) drove fire through a tube. A few years later the Mongols themselves used this weapon against the Europeans.

After that, in 1236, Ogadai let the insatiable Subotai lead an army westward to resume his earlier thrusts against that distant continent—Europe. Subotai pushed across Russia, overrunning the wooden-walled cities—including a

BIBLIOTHEQUE NATIONALE, SERVICE PHOTOGRAPHIQUE

A picture in History of the World shows a fortress being besieged by heavily armed Mongols who wear long tunics and peaked leather helmets with flaps over the ears.

small town called Moscow—into which the Russian princes shut themselves. On the Volga he was joined by Batu Khan, lord of the Western Tartars. Together in 1240 they crossed the frozen Dnieper River and leveled the beautiful old city of Kiev with its gilded domes and white walls. Fleeing westward, fugitives from the city carried word of the Mongol onslaught to the Hungarians.

In March, 1241, a Mongol spearhead drove into Poland and captured Cracow and other cities. Another column swung southeastward around the Carpathian Mountains, while the main body pushed right through the mountains and into Hungary. Before the Hungarians realized what had happened, the three columns had converged on the Danube and the city of Pest (later joined with its sister city, Buda, to form Budapest).

While petty princes in other European states quarreled

with each other or simply ignored the appeals of the Hungarian king, Bela IV, the pick of Eastern Europe's knights, barons, and men-at-arms marched out to confront the Mongol hordes. But the nomads on their shaggy ponies, like half-animal, half-human demons, drew away, feinted, struck, let the Europeans break through their ranks, and then cut them off, all with bewildering rapidity. Disorganized, the Europeans fled, the Mongols pursuing them mercilessly through marshes and woods, slaying seventy thousand men. One Mongol unit followed the fleeing King Bela to the eastern shores of the Adriatic, within striking distance of Marco Polo's Venice.

Then the people of Europe realized that the fearful reports they had been hearing for years were not exaggerated. The shock benumbed them. Misled by the Persian word for the Mongols, *Tatars*, and convinced that the Mongols were devils out of Tartarus (the hell of Greek mythology), they called the invaders Tartars—and shook with fear.

As one chronicler, Matthew Paris, referring to the year 1240, declared:

> In this year a detestable nation of Satan . . . broke loose from its mountain-environed home, and piercing the solid rocks [of the Caucasus], poured forth like devils. . . . They are thirsting for and drinking blood, tearing and devouring the flesh of dogs and men, dressed in oxhides, armed with plates of iron, thickset, strong, invincible.

In the spring of 1242, as the Mongols stood ready to strike deep into cowering Europe, Subotai and Batu suddenly ordered their armies to withdraw. Subotai hurried back to Mongolia while Batu retired to the gilded pavilions of his capital on the Volga. They never returned, and no man knows what devastation Venice and Europe were thereby spared.

The main reason for their turning back at this crucial moment was the news that the Great Khan Ogadai had died—of too much drinking, it is said; necessarily, they stopped fighting until a new great khan was elected. Certain historians have recently claimed, however, that the Mongols had gone as far as they wanted to go and were about to withdraw when Ogadai died.

After a period of dissension, during which various grandsons of Genghis Khan began to rule parts of the empire almost independently, Kuyuk, son of Ogadai, was elected Great Khan. He died after a short reign and was succeeded by another grandson of Genghis, Mangu. Although Mangu was as much interested in conquest as the great khans before him, he and his younger but more gifted brother Kublai were less brutal than the earlier great khans. Each tended to rely on reason rather than force in dealing with conquered peoples.

Still another grandson of Genghis, Hulagu, now led an army southwestward into Persia and gradually established himself as khan of the Levant, dominating an area from eastern Persia to the Mediterranean. It was he who sought out and destroyed the leader of the Assassins. It was he too who captured Baghdad, put to death its last caliph, slew ninety thousand of its inhabitants, and razed it so thor-

COLLECTION OF NATIONAL PALACE MUSEUM, CHINA

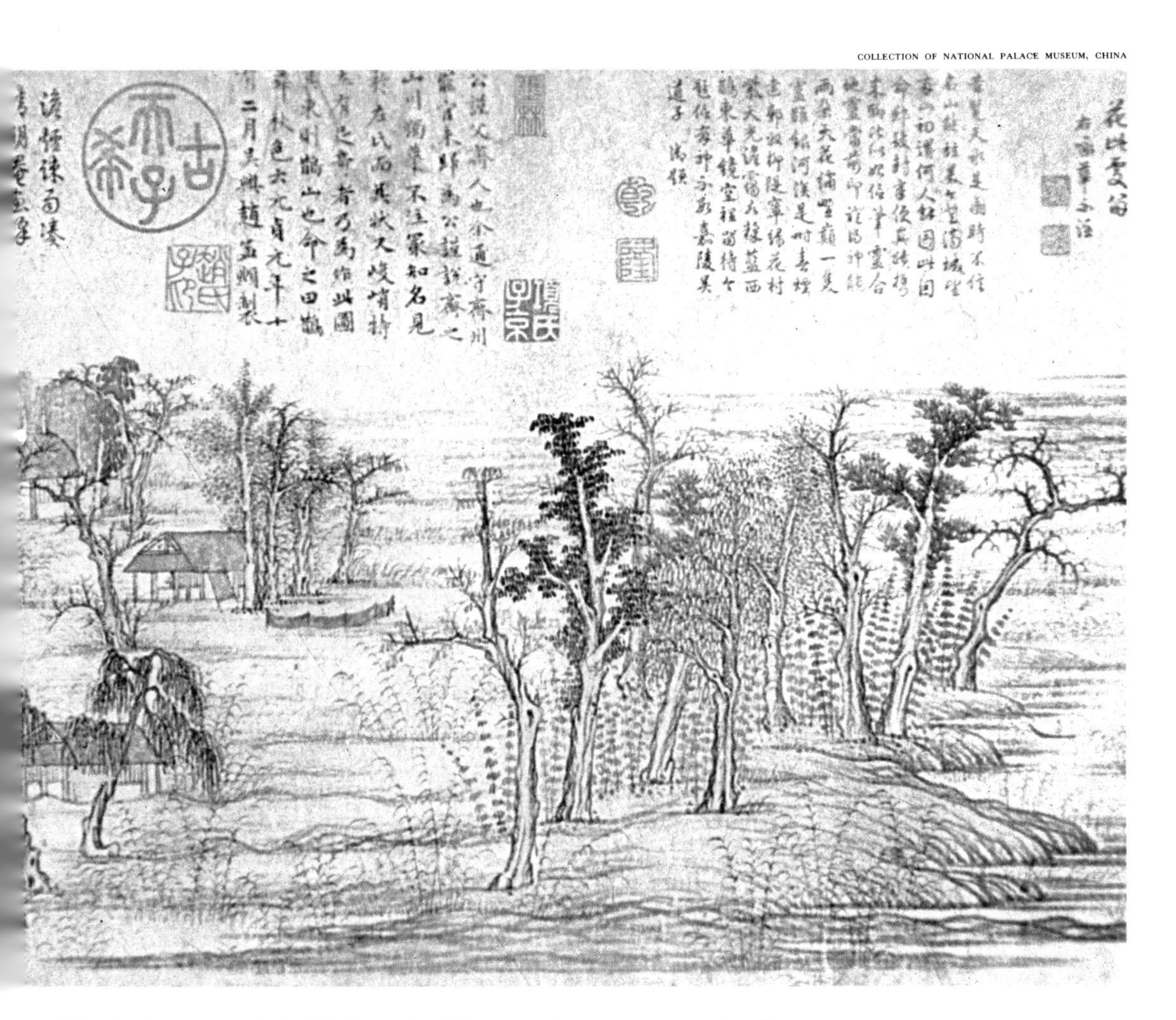

This landscape, marked with the seals of its several owners, was painted at about the time Marco was traveling through China. With its miniature fisherman and deer, the delicate scene appears strangely subdued and unreal.

oughly that many years passed before it regained any of its former glory. After that, Hulagu pushed farther westward. He was preparing to attack Egypt in 1259 when the death of Great Khan Mangu stopped what might have proved a history-making conquest. Hulagu decided to return to Mongolia to help choose a new great khan.

MUSEE GUIMET, PARIS: ARCHIVES PHOTOGRAPHIQUES

At the same time, Kublai—the brother of Mangu and Hulagu—who had been busy with an invasion of central China, quickly concluded a truce with the Chinese and hurried to his summer residence at Shangtu where he had his followers proclaim him Great Khan. His swift assumption of power resulted from his fear that his critics would elect his younger brother Arik Buka as Great Khan. Six years before, on his first campaign against China, other Mongol leaders had accused him of leniency, charging that he had been swayed by his Chinese tutors and advisers. It was true that the more time he spent in China, the more he became absorbed and fascinated by the country.

Kublai's fears had not been groundless. His younger brother had indeed been elected Great Khan in the Mongol capital of Karakorum. The rival claims were settled after a four-year war in which Arik Buka was defeated.

With his position firmly established, Kublai took a number of steps away from Mongol tradition. He had himself crowned Son of Heaven—the ancient title of the emperors of China—and transferred the court from Karakorum on the steppes to what is now the city of Peking near China's east coast. He dealt harshly with those chieftains who had opposed him, and although he expanded the empire, it was torn by discord and never recaptured the unity it had attained in earlier days. Seemingly, the Mongol Empire no sooner reached its peak than it began to disintegrate.

Kublai ascended the throne only thirty-three years after the death of Genghis Khan, but a profound change had already taken place in the character of the Mongol rulers. Where the first Great Khan had been a barbaric nomad as well as a ruthless conqueror, the new Great Khan was a highly civilized man who would develop into a wily rather than a strong ruler, a lover of refinement, elegance, and luxury. It was he who greeted the Polos and welcomed them to his domain.

Life in medieval China was marked by placidity and a regard for tradition. At right is a leisurely literary gathering. Above, two women serve tea. Although tea drinking was a common Chinese custom, Marco never mentions it.

The excitement of a dragon-boat regatta is captured in this silken handscroll. As oarsmen strain toward thei

COLLECTION OF NATIONAL PALACE MUSEUM, CHINA

rched on the prow of each boat swing flags, hoping to catch each other's flags and cut off opposing craft.

VI

KUBLAI'S COURT

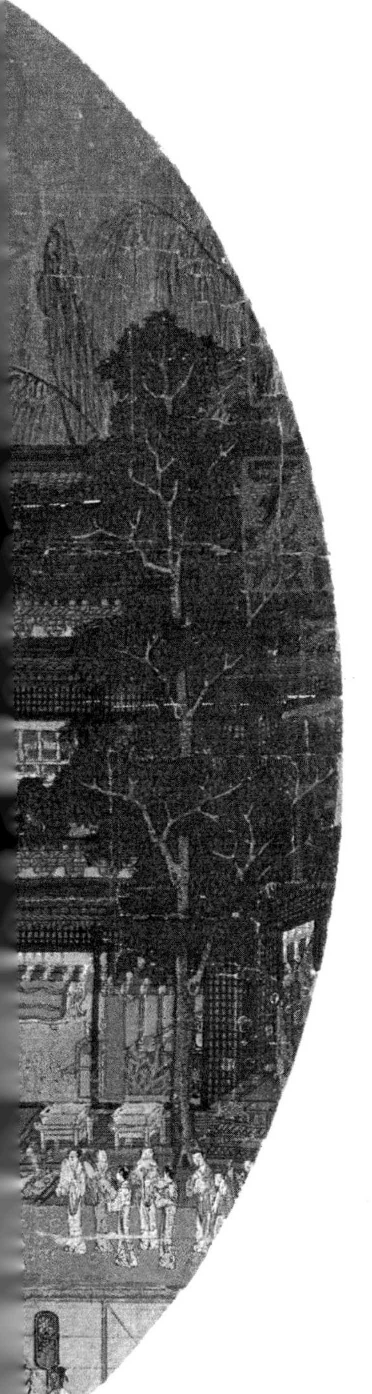

This painting of Chinese court life shows a palace brilliantly lighted at dusk. Court ladies climb to the tower at left to gaze at the moon.

Living, working, and traveling among the Chinese, young Marco quickly picked up their manners and customs. Noting the young Venetian's abilities and enthusiasm, Kublai soon began to send him on important missions. Indeed, Kublai preferred foreigners in official positions, partly because they were more familiar with complex problems of government than the Mongols and partly because he considered them more reliable than the Chinese—especially in governing China.

In the service of Kublai Khan, Marco gradually became one of his most trusted officers. Realizing that the Great Khan was fascinated by the customs of the peoples in his empire, Marco took notes constantly and turned routine reports into interesting narratives. Soon Kublai was letting him travel freely, enabling Marco to see more and more of the empire. And as Marco was taken increasingly into Kublai's confidence he had an unequaled opportunity to observe the Great Khan himself. Because of these advantages, Marco was able to leave a rich and fascinating picture of Chinese court and provincial life.

Although Kublai's admiration for the civilization of conquered China was great, he never lost his love for the two traditional Mongol pursuits—hunting and making war. For his hunting he created splendid parks. His summer palace at Shangtu, several hundred miles north and west of Peking, was set in the open country preferred by Mongols, but it was in most ways a work of Chinese art. Even Marco, who came from a rich European city, thought it incredibly luxurious. He describes the marble palace that served as the entrance to the park, which had sixteen miles of walls around it and was filled with deer and other animals. Here Kublai went hunting, usually with hawks but sometimes with small, half-tame cheetahs that rode on horses behind their keepers and which when loosed could quickly bring down game.

BIBLIOTHÈQUE NATIONALE, SERVICE PHOTOGRAPHIQUE

At the heart of the park was a pavilion of bamboo that had gilded columns topped by carved dragons. It was roofed with split halves of bamboo that had been waterproofed with lacquer. This airy structure was braced against the wind with two hundred strong silken cords, and the whole was so constructed that it could be taken down and set up again elsewhere.

Even when Kublai went hunting outside the park—as he did for several months every spring—it was under circumstances very different from the traditional nomad hunt. According to Marco, the monarch was accompanied by no less than ten thousand falconers who loosed the hawks and other hunting birds after the quarry; and ten thousand lookouts were so stationed that with their whistles they could call back the hunting birds and hood them. Because Kublai was almost sixty when Marco first met him and was already suffering from gout, he rode in a luxurious little cabin mounted on the backs of four elephants and draped with lion skins outside and lined with cloth of gold inside. When attendants warned him that such birds as cranes were approaching, he would draw back a curtain, and while reclining on a couch, watch the falcons swoop down and seize their prey.

For hunting deer the Great Khan had not only hundreds of packs of big dogs but trained cheetahs and lynxes. Even more unusual was Kublai's use of tigers to bring down boars, wild oxen, and bears. To prevent the tigers from becoming too ferocious when they were released, each was trained to live with a small dog. Strangest of all, however, were eagles that were taught to hunt wolves—as they still do in eastern Turkistan—by striking one claw into the wolf's back, another into its neck, and then with their beaks tearing out the animal's liver.

After the hunt, Kublai and his nobles would retire to a vast tent-city where their ladies awaited them and where

Here are two views of Kublai on a hunt: above, in a detail from a miniature in the French Book of Marvels, he rides a white horse with a trained cheetah lounging behind him; at right, in a work by the Mongol court painter Liu Kuan-tao, he is swathed in white ermine and attended by athletic courtiers.

COLLECTION OF NATIONAL PALACE MUSEUM, CHINA

CHATAIO
ha IX zoe 60.re de corona sotto
el suo dominio quando elva a
spasso el senta in un caro doro
e de avolio ornado de zoie el
presio dele qual e inextimabile
e questo caro vien menado da
uno elefante biancho, et ha mol
tire di piu nobili del suo regno
uno per canton che regeno questo caro, e li altri li vano avanti,
conassai numero de homeni
de armi davanti e da driedo e
quisono tut ti i piace-
ri e gentileze
e costumi
del mondo
Suzzazach
Quangu
Archanara
IMPERIO
e triumpho
nobilissimo
del chataio
chambalech
Iamin
IMPERIO
Sandu
A Questo gran tempio el qual e in
questo colfo concore gran parte de
questi orientali e qui i suo vodi e le
suo offerte. e per quelo se dice e qui
tanta assunanza de thesoro che
le quasi impossibile ad exti-
marlo.

the main tent, Marco claims, could hold at least a thousand persons. So they hunted in as much comfort as they enjoyed at home.

After spending the summer months in Shangtu, Kublai returned to his capital at Khanbalik ("City of the Great Khan"), where Peking is located today. Marco was overwhelmed by the splendor and size of the Mongol capital. Delightful as was Kublai's place at Shangtu, it was a summer fancy compared to the grandeur of Khanbalik.

The capital was twenty-four miles in circumference, and unlike any other city Marco had ever heard of, it was perfectly square and laid out like a chessboard. Instead of the narrow, twisting, alleylike passageways of medieval European cities, its streets were so straight and wide that one could look along them clear across the city. Many were lined with spacious houses, each having its own courtyard and garden. The outer walls of the city were at least forty-five feet high and more than forty-five feet wide at the base. To give some idea of the vast population of the city and its suburbs, Marco relates that the clothmakers had a thousand carts and pack horses loaded with raw silk brought in daily. Marco's figures seem exaggerated, but Khanbalik is known to have been larger than modern Peking; thus its needs were truly immense.

Within Khanbalik was a walled inner city containing the imperial palace, halls, and gardens. The palace walls were adorned with carved and gilded dragons and with paintings of birds, beasts, and men in battle. The roof, which was decorated in vermilion, azure, green, and violet, and then varnished, gleamed in the sun.

Not far from the palace was an artificial hill, over one hundred feet high and a mile around, which Kublai had caused to be planted with the most beautiful evergreens from all over the world. At the top of this hill, called the Green Mount, was a magnificent pavilion to which the Great Khan went to refresh his spirit. Surrounding the Green Mount was a large lake stocked with all kinds of fish for Kublai's table.

In separate buildings within the palace grounds dwelt Kublai's four wives; each was called empress and each had her own court. At the palace too lived his many concubines,

N.Y. PUBLIC LIBRARY, RARE BOOK DIVISION

KUBLA KHAN.

In Xanadu did Kubla Khan
A stately pleasure-dome decree:
Where Alph, the sacred river, ran
Through caverns measureless to man
Down to a sunless sea.
So twice five miles of fertile ground
With walls and towers were girdled round:
And here were gardens bright with sinuous rills
Where blossom'd many an incense-bearing tree;
And here were forests ancient as the hills,
And folding sunny spots of greenery.

But oh that deep romantick chasm which slanted
Down the green bill athwart cedarn cover!

One day in 1816, after reading about Marco's travels, the English poet Samuel Taylor Coleridge fell asleep and dreamed about what he had read. When he woke up, he transcribed the dream into a poem about Kublai Khan—in which the park at Shangtu is called Xanadu. One page from the poem is above.

At left is a nineteenth-century copy of a map made in 1459 and based on Marco's description of China. In the center is Kublai's palace at Khanbalik ("chambalech"), which the artist pictured as a Renaissance city.

who were selected at the rate of about thirty or forty every year from among the most beautiful young girls of Kungurat, a province famous for its handsome women. Each was carefully trained to serve the Great Khan, and he had so many that he would sometimes bestow one upon a noble as a reward. Far from being outraged at having their daughters chosen, parents considered it a piece of rare good fortune.

Among the spectacles that most dazzled Marco were Kublai's banquets, held in a hall that could seat six thousand guests. The Great Khan sat on a raised platform, and near him on an immense table was a huge vessel of pure gold brimming with wine and surrounded by large vessels of kumiss and other beverages. Kublai himself preferred the kumiss, which was made from the milk of a herd of immaculate white mares kept exclusively for him. So fastidious was he that each attendant who brought him a drink had to wear a silken cloth over his mouth lest his breath taint the liquor. As soon as Kublai raised his goblet to his lips, musicians began to play, and everyone knelt until the Great Khan had finished drinking. Although Marco does not say so, it is known that Kublai, like most Mongols, often drank to the point of drunkenness. When the banquet was over, musicians, tumblers, and jugglers entertained for the rest of the evening.

One annual festival, on September 28, celebrated the Khan's birthday; it was attended by twenty thousand nobles all dressed in cloth of gold. Some of these garments were gifts from Kublai and were adorned with gems and

COLLECTION OF NATIONAL PALACE MUSEUM, CHINA

In a scroll painting made three centuries before the Mongol conquest, ten court ladies gossip and drink their way through a concert. The lady at left with a fan and a large headdress may be the empress.

BIBLIOTHEQUE NATIONALE, SERVICE PHOTOGRAPHIQUE

This miniature from the Book of Marvels makes one of the Great Khan's lavish banquets seem an intimate, however formal, affair. Seated at center, Kublai receives four elegantly costumed noblemen who come before him bearing gifts.

pearls worth—so Marco declares—as much as 10,000 bezants (about $25,000). Perhaps it was this kind of report that later made his Venetian neighbors think he exaggerated wildly or even invented many of his reports. But scholars believe that Marco did not make up these stories and that his figures are in general quite reliable.

Another great court celebration was on New Year's Day. At this time it was customary for the Great Khan to receive gifts of gold, silver, precious stones, and fine horses from all over the empire. Sometimes he acquired as many as one hundred thousand horses, all white because that was considered a lucky color. In the pageant held that day there were as many as five thousand elephants, all bedecked in cloth embroidered with silk and gold. Afterward, the nobles, governors, and officials assembled in a great hall. As part of the ceremony, a dignitary rose and cried out four times, "Bow down and adore!" and each time everyone bent down until his forehead touched the floor in a ceremonial kowtow. Then they were all lavishly feasted and entertained.

The respect shown the Great Khan was extraordinary. Anyone coming within half a mile of the monarch was expected to lower his voice and assume a humble attitude.

PHILADELPHIA MUSEUM OF ART

WILLIAM ROCKHILL NELSON GALLERY OF ART

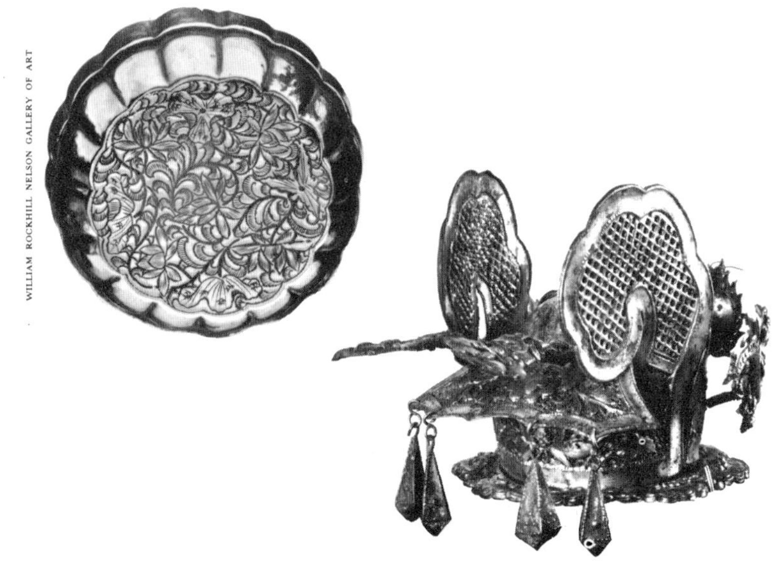

METROPOLITAN MUSEUM OF ART, ROGERS FUND, 1924

Treasures from every region of the empire flowed in as tribute to the Great Khan; and Marco, who had an eye for all that glittered, was dazzled. The kind of valuables that he loved to enumerate are shown here, from left to right: the engraved lid of a silver box, a silver headdress, two beautifully wrought ceramic vessels, and a silver-gilt crown set with jewels. The gold ewer above—a graceful pitcher encrusted with semi-precious stones—comes from a later period, that of the Ming dynasty.

If a man had an invitation to the palace, he took off his shoes and donned special white leather slippers before he entered; and in case he wished to spit he brought along a small lidded vessel for this purpose.

One feature of the Great Khan's government struck Marco as almost miraculous—paper currency. Although European merchants sometimes used promissory notes, and the Emperor Frederick II had tried issuing notes on leather, metal coins were the standard currency of Europe. So the Great Khan's power to give a piece of paper any value simply by stamping it seemed like an alchemist's dream of making gold. Describing how the paper money was made, Marco writes:

He [Kublai] has the bark stripped from mulberry trees . . . and takes from it that thin layer that lies between the coarser bark and the wood of the tree. This being steeped, and afterward pounded . . . until reduced to pulp, is made into paper, resembling that which is made from cotton . . . He has it cut into pieces of different sizes, nearly square, but somewhat longer than they are wide . . . To each note a number of officers . . . not only subscribe their names but also affix their seals . . . the principal officer, having dipped into vermilion the royal seal, stamps the piece of paper . . . Counterfeiting it is punished as a capital offense.

Surprisingly, Marco does not seem to have understood that the value of such currency depended on the store of gold that backed it up. He simply noted that it was wonderfully convenient for a foreign merchant to be able to exchange his cumbersome bags of strange coins for a few pieces of stamped paper. When the flimsy notes fell apart,

METROPOLITAN MUSEUM OF ART, FLETCHER FUND, 1937

METROPOLITAN MUSEUM OF ART
GIFT OF JOHN D. ROCKEFELLER JR., 1945

METROPOLITAN MUSEUM OF ART, FLETCHER FUND, 1934

the government mint rather greedily charged 3 per cent to exchange the old bills for new ones. It was not quite so perfect a device as Marco thought. Kublai nearly killed the goose that laid these golden eggs by issuing more and more paper with less and less reserves to back it up, until inflation set in and the bills lost most of their value. Marco thought that Kublai had originated such forms of money, but the Chinese had been using paper currency for more than two centuries.

Marco did overlook one vital aspect of the manufacture of paper currency—the fact that it was printed. Printing had been known in China since the ninth century; it did not appear in Europe before the fifteenth century. Marco was obviously so enchanted by the use of this money that he did not realize how important the printing itself was.

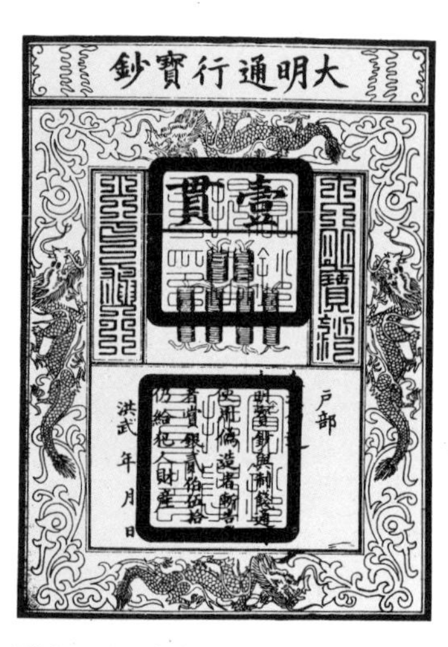

This unit of Chinese currency was printed a hundred years after Marco's visit. The bill is thought to be similar to those the Mongols used.

Almost as impressive to Marco as the paper money was the post, or courier, system—a Chinese forerunner of the pony express. It had been used in China for at least five hundred years, and the Mongols, like the Romans, made roads the nerve cords of their empire. At intervals of twenty-five or thirty miles on all the high roads across Asia were posthouses, or stations, called *yambs*. The *yambs* were spacious buildings, some having apartments furnished richly enough even for persons of the highest rank. Provisions and horses for most of these stations were furnished by the nearest village or town. At each station good horses—sometimes as many as 400—were kept in constant readiness for all official messengers or ambassadors. According to Marco, there were no fewer than 10,000 such buildings with at least 300,000 horses in the Great Khan's dominions. Here, for once, Marco himself doubted that Europeans would believe his figures.

Traveling from station to station at the rate of twenty-five or thirty miles a day, a rider could go great distances in a short time. But another arrangement provided even greater speed: every three miles between the *yambs*, a village of about forty houses supplied foot messengers to the post service. As a runner approached a station, the jingling of the bells he wore warned the next runner, as in a relay race, to be ready to take off. In case of an emergency, horses were also kept at the three-mile stations. Marco says that a special courier, galloping day and night, changing horses every three miles, and binding his waist, chest, and head with tight bands, could do as much as five hundred miles every twenty-four hours.

Still another wonder reported by Marco were black

PLIMPTON COLLECTION, COLUMBIA UNIVERSITY LIBRARIES

祕書郎以慶之勳重大明五年封文季爲山陽
縣五等伯轉太子舍人新安王北中郎主簿西
陽王撫軍功曹江夏王太祖東曹掾遷中書郎
慶之爲景和所殺兵仗圍宅收捕諸子文季長
兄文叔謂文季曰我能死爾能報遂自縊文季
揮刀馳馬去收者不敢追遂得免明帝立起文
季爲寧朔將軍遷太子右衞率建安王司徒
司馬赭圻平爲宣威將軍廬江王太尉長史出
爲寧朔將軍征北司馬廣陵太守轉黃門郎領
長水校尉明帝宴會朝臣以南臺御史賀臧爲
柱下史糾不醉者文季不肯飲酒被驅下殿晉
平王休祐爲南徐州帝問褚淵須幹事人爲上
佐淵舉文季轉寧朔將軍驃騎長史南東海太
守休祐被殺雖用蕃禮僚佐多不敢至文季獨
往省墓展哀出爲臨海太守元徽初遷散騎常侍
領後軍將軍轉祕書監出爲吳興太守文季飲
酒至五斗妻王氏王錫女飲酒亦至三斗文季
與對飲竟日而視事不廢昇明元年沈攸之反

The Chinese were printing books long before movable type was first used in Europe. These pages are from a history book that may have been printed in the tenth century.

stones that burned. He describes how these were mined and how they could keep burning from evening till the following morning. The Chinese had need of a great deal of fuel, he explains, because they took hot baths three times a week in summer and daily in winter, and every wealthy family had a stove and a bath of its own. To Venetians, Marco's tale of daily baths in winter must have seemed almost as unbelievable as that of black stones that burned all night.

According to Marco, Kublai was a benevolent despot. When storms, blight, or locusts ruined farmers' crops, he excused the victims from paying taxes and gave them grain for sowing as well as for food. To provide for periods of scarcity he stored huge quantities of grain in times of plenty. When misfortune struck a family, he would insist that it be given as much food and clothing as it had had the year before. Homeless children were taken up and educated, and many hospitals were established. And every day his officers distributed thirty-five thousand bowls of rice and millet to the needy—a great departure from the Mongol belief that the poor were accursed and should be driven away.

Asserting that those who gambled did so with his property, Kublai forbade what he called "all such forms of

cheating." He completed the Grand Canal, which ran from Peking to Hangchow, a tremendous achievement. And for the sake of beauty as well as shade, he had trees planted along both sides of every major highway.

Because Kublai himself was curious and inquiring, he encouraged certain sciences. Although Marco does not mention the fact, it is known that the Great Khan erected a splendid observatory for his astrologers and astronomers. His tolerance in religious matters was also remarkable, even though it may have come from cunning rather than broadmindedness. At Easter and Christmas he had the Christian Bible brought to him and he kissed it reverently, but he also respected the holy days of the Saracens, Jews, and Buddhists. When he was asked why he did so, he replied:

> There are four great prophets who are reverenced . . . by the different classes of mankind. The Christians regard Jesus Christ as their divinity; the Saracens, Mohammed; the Jews, Moses; and the idolaters, Buddha . . . I do honor and show respect to all four so that I may be sure of invoking whichever among them is in truth supreme in heaven.

Although Marco thought that Kublai mainly favored Christianity, the Great Khan was really most impressed by the Buddhist lamas. He believed that the Christians were no match for the Buddhists at his court, especially with respect to feats of wizardry. These wizards, or magicians, came mostly from Tibet. Marco relates that they could stop a storm or make a goblet of wine fly across the hall from a serving table to Kublai's hand and then back again after he had emptied it.

Having seen the power and magnificence of the Great Khan's court, Marco had reason to be pleased when Kublai chose him to make an inspection tour of the provinces. Marco's first mission took him into Yunnan province, which was about a four months' journey southwest from the capital. Marco made the most of this opportunity, going as far as the border of Tibet in the west and Burma in the south. Along with his report on the province and its officials, he brought back the kind of vivid details of the countryside and the customs of the people that he knew would interest the Great Khan.

The country he passed through ranged from fertile valleys to craggy mountains. There were waterways such

The perils and the scenic beauty of mountain travel in China can be seen in this scroll painting.

BODLEIAN LIBRARY, OXFORD

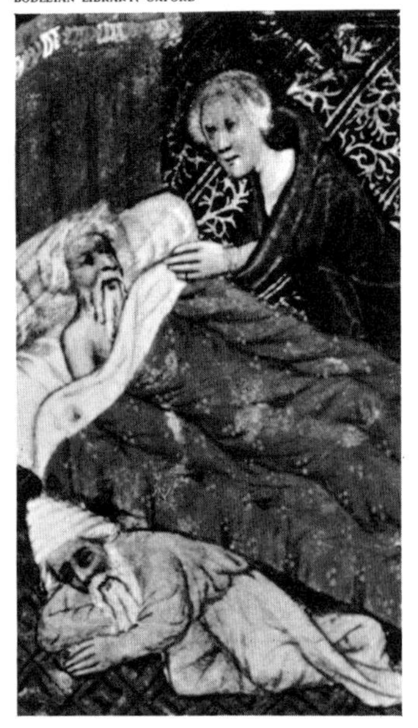

Marco tells of the Burmese custom of couvade, *in which the father stays in bed after a child is born. This illustration of the practice also shows a man sleeping by the bed.*

as the Kinsha-kiang, known as the River of Golden Sands, and a mountain range so rugged that it could be crossed only by a narrow road that crept along the side of towering cliffs; in many places the road was held up on the outer edge only by wooden supports.

The people were as varied as the terrain: from dwellers in thriving cities to poor, half-wild tribesmen. There was, on the one hand, the so-called Golden King, attended by beautiful girls who even drew him around his estate in a little carriage, and the king of Burma, who built himself two pagodas, one plated with gold and the other with silver. On the other hand, there were primitive people who used cowrie shells for money; those who called in devil dancers to drive the evil spirits from the bodies of persons who became ill; and still others who dipped needles in dark coloring matter, and painfully puncturing the skin, tattooed their bodies with pictures of flowers and beasts.

Even more curious was the custom of a tribe on the Burmese border. When a baby was born there, the father would go to bed with it for forty days while the mother waited on him and the baby. The tribesmen believed this practice would establish a sympathetic bond between the father and child. Topsy-turvy as this custom may seem, sociologists say it has been a custom among various peoples in many parts of the world. Oddest of all were the people who murdered any visiting stranger who had qualities they admired, believing that his spirit—and his qualities—would remain with the family in whose house he was slain.

Although Marco himself reached Burma a year or so after the event, he vividly describes the battle that occurred in 1277 when the king of Burma and Bengal tried to stop a Mongol invasion by using an army of elephants against it. Each elephant bore on its back a wooden battlement holding about a dozen men. The Mongol commander had only twelve thousand troops as against sixty thousand Burmese, but he was an experienced and wily general, and he faced the Burmese confidently. He made sure only that he had dense woods close by. When the Burmese forces pressed forward, the Mongol horses were terrified by the elephants. The Mongols immediately dis-

TEXT CONTINUED ON PAGE 112

As an emissary of Kublai, Marco traveled south from Khanbalik, and crossing the Yangtze River, went through Yunnan to the kingdom's southern limit. The Polos had entered the kingdom along China's northern border.

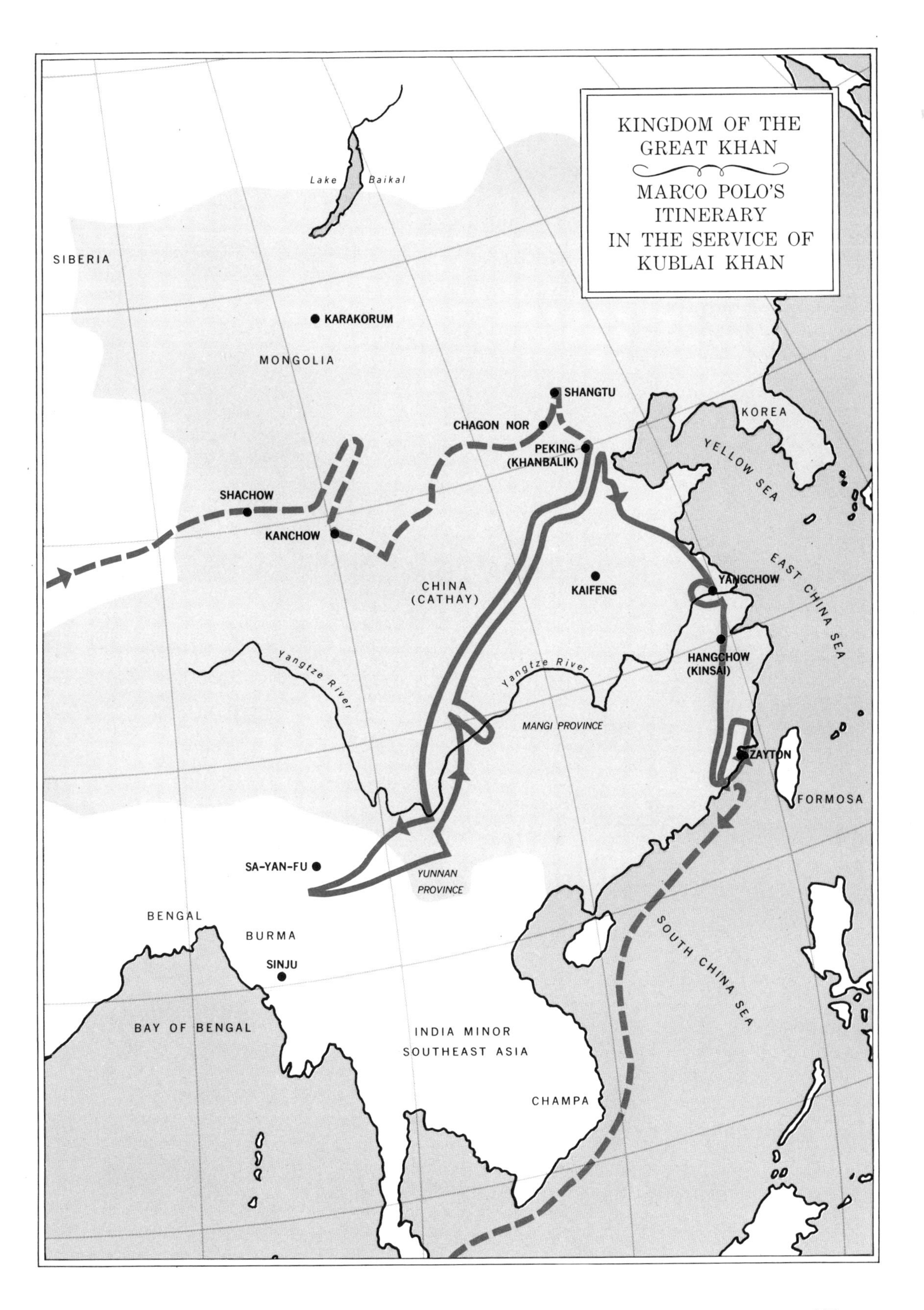
KINGDOM OF THE GREAT KHAN
MARCO POLO'S ITINERARY IN THE SERVICE OF KUBLAI KHAN
Lake Baikal
SIBERIA
KARAKORUM
MONGOLIA
SHANGTU
CHAGON NOR
PEKING (KHANBALIK)
KOREA
YELLOW SEA
SHACHOW
KANCHOW
EAST CHINA SEA
CHINA (CATHAY)
KAIFENG
YANGCHOW
HANGCHOW (KINSAI)
Yangtze River
Yangtze River
MANGI PROVINCE
ZAYTON
FORMOSA
SA-YAN-FU
YUNNAN PROVINCE
BENGAL
BURMA
SINJU
SOUTH CHINA SEA
BAY OF BENGAL
INDIA MINOR SOUTHEAST ASIA
CHAMPA

Vendors, sidewalk salesmen with their thronging customers, and scribes fill this busy street scene painted sho

r Marco's arrival in China: The stallman at right above is selling masks, pin wheels, and other knickknacks.

BODLEIAN LIBRARY, OXFORD

The French manuscript, Book of the Great Khan, *portrayed the siege of Sa-yan-fu as if it were a battle in Europe with cannon, crossbows, and knights in armor.*

TEXT CONTINUED FROM PAGE 108

mounted, and with their powerful bows drove so many arrows into the elephants that the huge beasts ran off into the nearby woods, brushing the men and fortresses from their backs. Then the Mongols remounted their horses, put the enemy to rout, and slew them as they fled. The Mongol commander later had some of the elephants rounded up, and thereafter Kublai Khan always included troop-carrying elephants in his armies.

Marco's second important mission took him into Mangi,

an immense and stubbornly independent province in the southeast of China, which Marco describes as the richest province in the Eastern world. Shortly before this, Kublai's General Bayan had put down all remaining resistance in Mangi and forced the boy emperor, last of the Sung dynasty, and his grandmother, the regent, to acknowledge Mongol domination. When the child and his grandmother heard that their conquerors would not kill or humiliate them, they turned toward the north, kowtowed in Kublai's direction, and dutifully recognized him as the new Son of Heaven.

It was in Yangchow, one of the foremost cities of Mangi, that, Marco declares, he served as governor. Since his name does not appear on the official Chinese list of governors of the city, it is thought that he was not actually the governor but probably something like Kublai's chief personal representative. Whatever position Marco may have held, it is surprising that he tells us little about the city and nothing whatever about his own experiences there.

Another report by Marco that does not seem to agree with historical records is his description of the siege of Sa-yan-fu and its final surrender to the Mongol armies. So strong were the defenses of this city that it withstood a heavy siege for five years. Marco writes that upon hearing of the city's resistance, Nicolo and Maffeo Polo offered to build mangonels, slinglike machines used in Europe for hurling huge stones and other objects into a besieged city. Marco goes on to say that the brothers actually supervised the construction of the mangonels, and setting them up, hurled several three-hundred pound stones into the city, crushing many buildings. Terrified by what seemed like thunderbolts from nowhere, the inhabitants immediately surrendered, and the Venetians received much of the credit for the victory. Although Marco recounts the event vividly, it is questionable whether the Polos participated in the siege. Sa-yan-fu was finally taken in 1273; most scholars believe the Polos reached China in 1275.

With considerably more accuracy, Marco describes the Yangtze, one of the world's great rivers. To him it looked in some places like a sea, and he was stunned by the number of ships he saw on it. He estimated that there were 15,000 vessels, each between 200 and 500 tons burden, at the city of Sinju alone. He explains how they were tracked, or towed, upstream by teams of horses that plodded along the bank, the animals being attached to the boat by a long rope.

But the high point of all of Marco's descriptions of

COURTESY OF THE SMITHSONIAN INSTITUTION, FREER GALLERY OF ART, WASHINGTON, D.C.

Chinese life is that of the city of Kinsai (modern Hangchow). Marco says that Kinsai was 100 miles in circumference and that it contained 1,600,000 families. Located between a magnificent lake and a great river, it had an immense number of canals; like Venice, it was as easy for one to get around by water as by land. According to Marco, it had 12,000 bridges, many of them arched so high that tall masts could pass under them but not so steep as to prevent carts from crossing over them.

Accustomed to one central market in Venice, Marco was surprised to find that Kinsai had markets in ten main squares, each half a mile long and half a mile wide. On three days every week some forty to fifty thousand persons passed through each market. These markets carried every kind of meat, fish, fruit, fowl, and herb, and in the shops around the squares one could buy any article from a trinket to a pearl. To give some idea of the stupendous amount of food consumed by the city, Marco declares that almost ten thousand pounds of pepper were brought into it each day.

In the streets near the markets were the public baths, which the inhabitants considered very healthful. Many physicians and astrologers also dwelt nearby, the latter not only foretelling the future from the stars but giving lessons in reading and writing. The city had twelve guilds representing twelve different crafts. According to Marco, each guild had twelve thousand workshops, and each shop employed from twelve to forty artisans. These guilds supplied goods and articles for Kinsai as well as other cities throughout China.

The masters of these shops were so rich that they did no work themselves but spent much of their time strutting proudly about. Their wives also avoided work, dressing themselves in costly garments and putting on delicate and languid airs. These merchants lavished much money on their homes, decorating them with carvings, paintings, and ornaments of every kind.

Marco found the inhabitants of Kinsai not only peace-loving, but honest in business, friendly to each other, and cordial to strangers. Their daughters were modest and demure, and the young men were well behaved.

Most of the houses of Kinsai were made of wood and

Eminent personages carried in palanquins or shaded by parasols glide along the avenue in the foreground of this fourteenth-century view of Kinsai. On the far shore of the lake are some of the magnificent homes Marco describes.

caught fire easily, but Marco was continually impressed by the efficiency of the fire-fighting system. It consisted of watchmen on every main bridge. When one sighted a fire, he sounded an alarm by beating on wooden drums, whereupon the watchmen from all nearby bridges came running to help put out the fire. These watchmen also patrolled the streets at curfew to see that all lights and fires were out and that no one was abroad without reason.

All the streets of Kinsai were paved with stone and brick, and the grandest was about one hundred feet wide. Elegant vehicles, curtained and cushioned in silk, went to and fro on this thoroughfare all day long.

For Marco the most beautiful feature of the city was the immense lake whose edge was planted with trees and surrounded by handsome homes and temples. In the middle of the lake were two islands on which stood sumptuous, completely furnished pavilions that any citizen could use for a wedding celebration, banquet, or other entertainment. Sometimes there would be a hundred such parties going on at once; and these pavilions were maintained entirely by the city. There were also many large pleasure vessels with comfortable, richly adorned cabins. After business hours, the residents of the city flocked to the lake to spend hours sitting at tables on these vessels and enjoying the beauty of the passing scene.

Marco obviously thought that Kinsai was so wonderful because of its well-paved streets and good markets, its efficient watchmen, its fine carriages and pleasure vessels, and its other comforts. He did not see that it was even more admirable as one of the greatest centers of culture, of education and the arts, that the world had ever known; there were at that time more books in its libraries than in any other city in China.

But after the Mongol conquest in 1279—only a short time after the Polos arrived—China began to stagnate. Although Kublai was a shrewd and able ruler, he was nonetheless a foreign conqueror, and the Chinese for a hundred years were a conquered people. Even after the Ming dynasty finally expelled the Mongols in 1371, China never recovered its greatness. Marco therefore had the unique good fortune to see Kinsai and much of China at the peak of their glory.

Few details of Chinese life escaped Marco's eyes. He would have seen many overloaded peddlers such as this one pictured by an artist in the 1200's.

COLLECTION OF NATIONAL PALACE MUSEUM, CHINA

The Polos set sail from the seaport of Zayton in the illustration above from a French manuscript. Their boat is strangely small, and the artist did not know how the rigging should be tied to the bow. But the spirit of the scene seems appropriate—a seaman on a nearby merchant ship is blowing a farewell blast on his trumpet. The detail at right from a fifteenth-century map shows "Zaiton" as a city of spires at the head of an inlet.

VII

HOMEWARD BY SEA

Seventeen years passed before the Polos began to think of returning home. It was then 1291, and the elder Polos had been home only once in thirty-seven years. Furthermore, Kublai was seventy-five years old, and the Polos realized that if he should die, jealous people at the court could make life difficult for them. There were many reasons why they may not have thought of leaving sooner: they were kept busy, the world they lived in was full of endless wonders, they were well rewarded for their work, and they were privileged persons.

However, when Nicolo begged Kublai to let them go home, the Great Khan seemed hurt and could not understand why they should be so eager to make such a dangerous journey once again. If it was wealth they wanted, he promised he would give them double whatever they possessed and all the honors they might desire. But surely one of the main reasons for his attitude was the fact that the Polos, and especially Marco, had proved such valuable and faithful lieutenants.

Then chance brought the Polos a totally unexpected opportunity. Bolgana, the favorite wife of Arghun, Khan of Persia, had died but had left a wish that her successor be chosen from her kindred in Mongolia. So in 1286 Arghun had dispatched three envoys to Khanbalik with a request that Kublai send him a new wife from among the women of Bolgana's family.

Kublai chose the Princess Cocachin, a lovely and accomplished seventeen-year-old, to fill Bolgana's place. The three envoys and Cocachin started on their long trip to Persia. But war had broken out among the Mongol tribes along the caravan routes of Central Asia, and after eight wearisome months on the road, the company had to return to Khanbalik. At that point Marco had just come back from a successful mission by sea to India. Hearing of this, the Persian envoys proposed that he help them reach Persia by water. Seeing an opportunity to return home himself, Marco gladly agreed. The envoys promptly presented the plan to the Great Khan. Kublai was at first displeased but finally yielded.

Once he had given way, however, he spoke to the Polos in the friendliest manner. He appointed them his missionaries to the pope and to the kings of Europe and gave them the imperial gold tablet that guaranteed them safe passage. He may also have presented them with many rubies and other jewels. Finally, he directed that they be allowed thirteen ships and be supplied with stores and provisions for at least two years.

Marco was much impressed by the vessels. Great four-masters with as many as sixty cabins below deck, they were larger and more comfortable than comparable European ships. They were sheathed in a double layer of planking, fastened with iron nails, and calked with oakum. And since the Chinese had no pitch, the boats were coated on the bottom with a paste of quicklime, chopped hemp, and tung oil. Marco was especially struck by the way the interior was divided by bulkheads into small, watertight compartments. If a whale, he points out, attracted at night by the glitter of the ship's wake, rammed the vessel, the crew

REPRODUCTION COURTESY OF JAMES CAHILL, FREER GALLERY OF ART

BIBLIOTHEQUE NATIONALE, SERVICE PHOTOGRAPHIQUE

The vessel in the center of the twelfth-century river scene at left was sturdy and commodious enough for coastwise travel. Some of the cabin occupants have opened their shutters. Princess Cocachin, who sailed with the Polos, was to marry Arghun, the Khan of Persia, shown above in his garden.

could confine the water to one compartment, remove the cargo from it, and repair the damage. This safety measure was not introduced into European vessels until the nineteenth century. The largest of these Chinese vessels had crews of two to three hundred men and carried tenders to help when the ships were being rowed; in addition they had several smaller boats for fishing, paying out the anchor, and other work. The captain of such a vessel was treated with almost royal ceremony.

Zayton, the great port from which the convoy was to sail, was on the South China Sea. At this point, Marco tells the history of a certain very large island off the coast of China—Japan (or Zipangu, as it was called). Marco never reached Japan, but perhaps because of the many stories he had heard about it, and because it was completely unknown in Europe, he devotes a number of pages to it. He greatly exaggerates the wealth of this island chain, asserting that its supply of gold was inexhaustible and that the emperor's palace had a golden roof and a floor containing small slabs of pure gold. Japan was also rich in precious stones, he says, and had so many pearls of a large pink kind that the inhabitants put one into the mouth of each corpse as part of the burial rite.

This is one of the sections of the *Travels* that is not firsthand and not reliable. Ironically, it was such descriptions that two centuries later provided fuel for the hopes and schemes of Christopher Columbus. Relying on some of Marco's estimates, Toscanelli, the geographer whose map Columbus used, placed Japan about six or seven thousand miles to the west of Portugal. Japan is not only more than twice that distance from Europe, but the continent of North America lies in between.

Marco also tells how Kublai tried to conquer Japan. According to Marco's story, the Mongols landed on one of the islands, but their fleet was driven off by a storm. The 30,000 men who were left on the shore, he says, captured a nearby city but were forced to surrender after being blockaded for six months. The historical fact is that in 1275 Kublai sent one fleet with Mongol and Korean forces, but it was quickly repulsed. So in 1281 he sent a combined task force made up of 40,000 Mongols and Koreans, together with another army of 100,000 Chinese and Mongols. They established a beachhead on the island of Kyushu but were held down by local resistance. Then a storm struck the fleet (said to number 4,000 vessels) and drove it onto the rocks. Only 200 of the ships escaped, and the invaders who

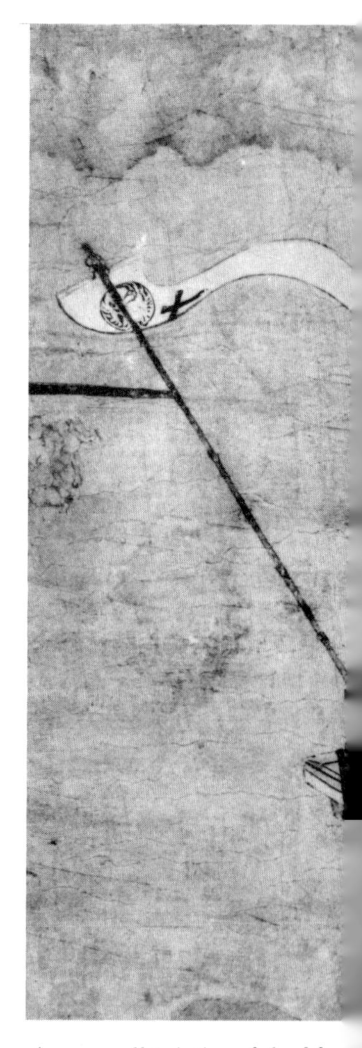

A rare scroll painting of the Mon-gols' unsuccessful invasion of Japa- depicts Kublai's warriors as fren-zied pirates and his landing cra- as high-sterned and unseaworth-

MUSEE GUIMET, PARIS

were left stranded were killed or enslaved. The ever-loyal Marco explains Kublai's failure as the result first of a quarrel between the two generals who commanded the joint task force and second of the unexpected storm. But Kublai's crucial mistake was his attempt to make war in a situation where his men did not have their horses and could not maneuver freely.

Marco adds that when the natives of Japan captured an enemy who could not raise a ransom, they killed and cooked him, inviting all their friends to the feast. They claimed that human flesh had a better flavor than any other.

The convoy of the Polos and the Princess Cocachin, carrying at least two thousand persons in all, left Zayton early in the spring of 1292. After two months of sailing

BIBLIOTHEQUE NATIONALE, SERVICE PHOTOGRAPHIQUE

BODLEIAN LIBRARY, OXFORD

southwestward, they came to Champa (in Indochina), a kingdom whose monarch paid Kublai an annual tribute of twenty elephants and much sweet-scented aloeswood. As the ships then made their way among the great islands of the East Indies, Marco was impressed at many places, and especially at Java, by the busy trade in spices and gold. If these islands had not been situated so far across the seas from China, he adds, the Great Khan would have surely overrun them all.

Early travelers had a rather limited knowledge of navigation, as is evident from Marco's comment that their convoy was so far south they could no longer see the North Star. Actually they were never more than one degree from the equator, and the North Star was visible, but very low on the horizon. Apparently Marco did not know where to look for it.

Sea travel was not only uncertain but agonizingly slow. The expedition was delayed for five months in Sumatra because no vessel could set out on the long voyage to Ceylon while the southwest monsoon was blowing against it.

The natives of the coast of Sumatra were man-eating savages, so when Marco set up a camp on shore, he had a ditch dug and guards posted around it. After a while the natives became friendly and began to supply the camp with food, including "nuts as large as a man's head" and wine that came from a palm tree. From this—and Marco's further comment that there was also a tree here that yielded a flour suitable for making bread and cakes—it can be understood why some of his neighbors in Venice later thought that his descriptions were all a braggart's exaggerations, typical "travelers' tales." But the savages of northern Sumatra were really cannibals (and remained so up into the present century); the giant nuts were coconuts, which Europeans had never seen; the wine was drawn from the gomuti, or toddy, palm; and the flour was sago, and it did come from the pith of a tree.

However, when Marco writes about people that he himself did not see, he sometimes mixes fable with fact—as when he speaks of a hill tribe in Sumatra with tails like those of dogs.

Marco probably did not stop at Java to see the black pepper-pickers pictured at left above. And it is not likely that the pearl divers of Ceylon actually presented baskets of pearls to the Polos. But early artists who illustrated Marco's travels did their best to portray places he described.

The convoy finally crossed the immense stretch of open sea to Ceylon, which must have been the most perilous portion of the voyage. But Marco speaks only of the huge rubies for which Ceylon was known. He relates that one ruby owned by the king was almost as big as a man's fist; to buy it Kublai had offered the value of an entire city, but the king had refused to sell it.

It was also near Ceylon, in the shallow waters off the Indian coast, that the voyagers came upon a strange kind of fishing—that of the pearling fleet. Marco was especially interested in the divers who kept going down to six-fathom depths all day long, each time collecting as many oysters as they could. The oysters were later opened and set in tubs of water; when they had rotted sufficiently, the soft parts would float to the top while the pearls remained at the bottom.

Since the waters were infested with sharks, the merchants took a most unusual measure to protect the divers. They hired certain enchanters of the Brahman class who could supposedly cast a spell that would stupefy the dangerous fish while the divers were at work. The wizards withdrew the charm at night so that outsiders who tried to dive for the pearls would not be protected. (Apparently both divers and merchants thought the spells worked because the enchanters continued to be employed for centuries.) Pearl fishing took place in April and May, at the end of which time the stock of oysters at this place was exhausted and the pearling fleet went elsewhere.

Here Marco relates one of the most valuable stories in his book—that of the life of Sagamoni Borcan (the Mongol name for Sakyamuni), the Indian prince who became the Buddha and founded the great religion of Buddhism. Although the prince actually lived in northern India, Marco sets the story in Ceylon because the islanders declared that the Buddha had been born there and that his body was entombed on the island's highest mountain. Marco reported that relics of the Buddha could still be seen on the mountain.

The story Marco heard was that Sagamoni Borcan was the son of a king of the island. From childhood on he showed a dedication to holy things and had no interest in becoming king or in acquiring any worldly possessions. His father tempted him with beautiful girls and other pleasures, but the youth could not be swerved. The king also sought to keep him from all knowledge of old age and death. But one day the youth came upon an aged and decrepit man; when he insisted on knowing why the old man looked as he did, the prince discovered the truth. He re-

METROPOLITAN MUSEUM OF ART, PURCHASE, 1934, JOSEPH PULITZER BEQUEST

Buddhism, the major Asiatic religion that Marco Polo encountered in Ceylon, numbers many gods and saints among its revered figures. One of them is Kuan-yin, the goddess of mercy, who was sculpted by many Oriental artists in the Middle Ages. This Chinese figure of the goddess shows her poised, as if listening, on a half-open lotus.

turned home more than ever convinced that the pleasures of life were meaningless.

So one night he stole away and went up on a lofty mountain, and there he lived like a holy hermit until he died. The grief-stricken father, Marco was told, had an image of his son fashioned of gold and precious stones, and he required all his subjects to worship it as a god. After Sagamoni Borcan died, he was reborn first as an ox, then as a horse, until after eighty-four incarnations in animal forms, he became a god superior to all other gods.

Pilgrims came from everywhere, Marco adds, to see the relics of the Buddha—his teeth, his bowl, and some of his hair—preserved on the mountain. In 1284 Kublai himself sent a mission to secure one of the Buddha's teeth.

The important thing about Marco's story is that it was sympathetic; for some reason Marco was not so prejudiced against this religion as he was against the Moslem faith. The Buddha, he declares, would have become a saint if he had been a Christian. And thus one of the first accounts Europe had of the Buddha was that he was the noble founder of a great religion.

Reaching India, Marco was fascinated by the country

The Buddha, wreathed in incense and seated on a lotus throne, is worshiped by Mongolian royalty in this tenth-century scroll painting.

and its people. He thought it the richest and most splendid province on earth, and he describes its opulence two centuries before Vasco da Gama was credited with opening it up to Europeans. Writing first of the Coromandel Coast, he says that no tailors lived there because it never became cold, and everyone wore only a breechcloth. Even the king used no other garment, but was bedecked with priceless ornaments, including a collar of diamonds, a necklace of 104 pearls and rubies (one jewel for each time he must repeat a certain prayer daily), gold bracelets on his arms and legs, and rings on his fingers and toes. Besides five hundred wives, a great many barons accompanied the king wherever he went. When he died and was cremated, these men threw themselves into the fire in order to follow him into the next life.

Such was the religious zeal of certain other Hindus that they often sacrificed themselves to idols. First, writes Marco, the friends of such a fanatic bore him through the streets, proclaiming what he was about to do. Then, in front of the idol, the fanatic plunged dagger after dagger into his arms, legs, stomach, and breast, crying to the idol with each thrust, "I sacrifice myself in honor of such an idol." Finally,

PERMISSION OF THE TRUSTEES OF THE BRITISH MUSEUM

In India, Marco learned about yogis, a sect of Hindus who fast and who mortify their bodies as proof of their complete devotion to God.

COURTESY THE CLEVELAND MUSEUM OF ART

he plunged the last of the daggers into his heart and fell dead. Marco was so astonished by this performance that he assumed these men were criminals condemned to death who had chosen to take their own lives. But they were simply religious zealots.

Equally astonishing was the custom wherein a wife whose husband had died was expected to cast herself on his funeral pyre. Many women did so (but it is said that some had to be drugged first) and were much honored; those who did not do so were scorned. This ancient and cruel practice, called *suttee*, was not outlawed in India until the nineteenth century.

In Europe people rarely washed themselves, but in India it was part of the daily ritual. The natives washed their entire bodies both morning and evening before eating. Each individual had his own drinking vessel and would not use one belonging to any other person. So fastidious were they that a drinker did not put his lips to a vessel but held it above his head and poured the liquid into his mouth.

Criminals were strictly punished. Creditors had a unique way of dealing with a debtor. The creditor would draw a circle around the debtor, who then could not leave until he had satisfied the creditor. Marco himself saw a bold use of this procedure. A merchant who had been unable to collect a debt from a king met the monarch out riding on horseback and managed to draw a circle around him and his horse. The king immediately halted, and acknowledging the justness of the claim, would not move on until the man had been paid.

TEXT CONTINUED ON PAGE 134

METROPOLITAN MUSEUM OF ART, GIFT OF THE SHAW FOUNDATION, INC., 1959

After leaving Zayton, the Polos sailed through the South China Sea to Sumatra and thence to Ceylon and India, making note of all the wonders, real and legendary, along the way. The marvelous jeweled camel at left was crafted in India.

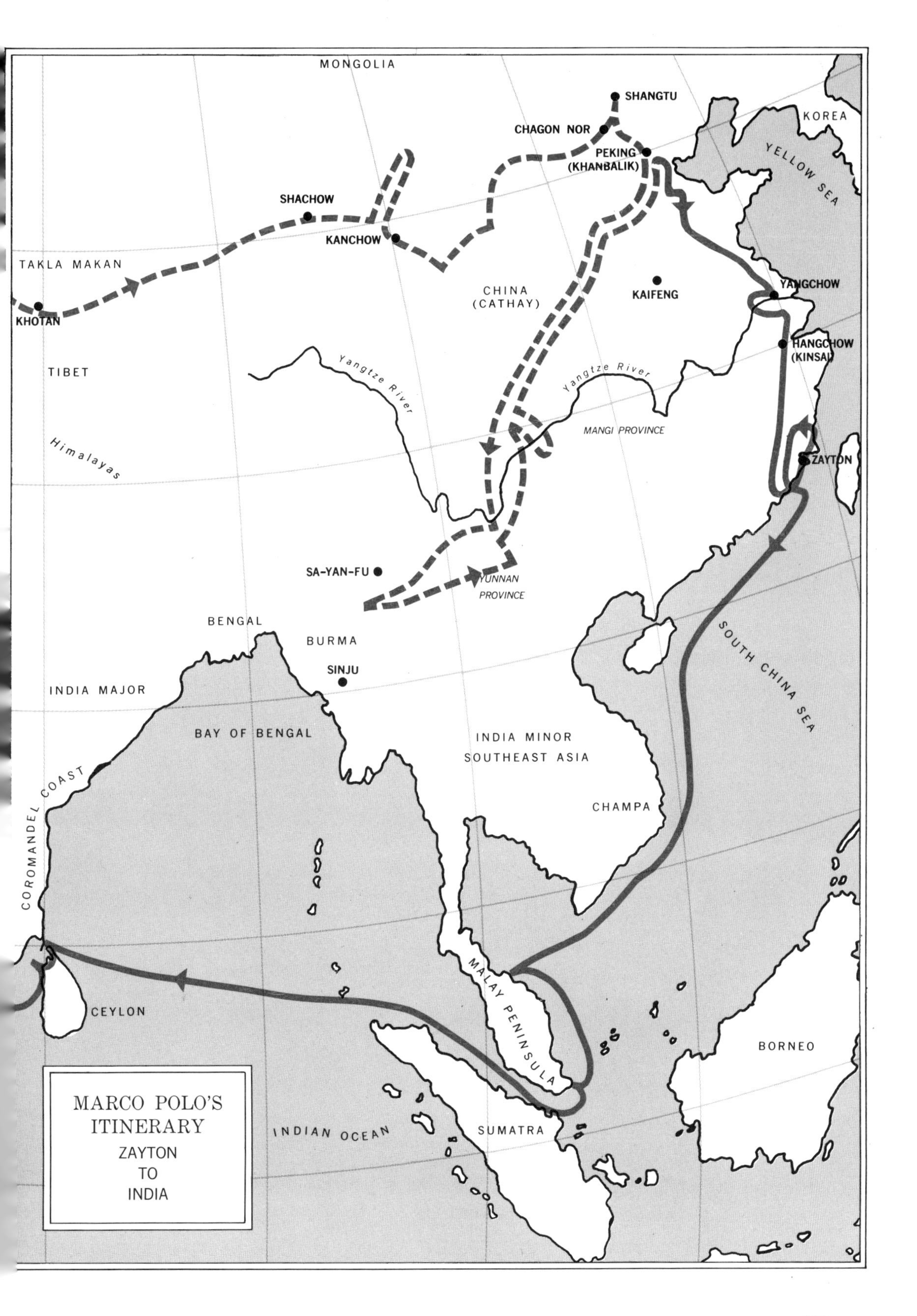

MARCO POLO'S ITINERARY

ZAYTON TO INDIA

METROPOLITAN MUSEUM OF ART, ROGERS FUND, 1925

The Indian princes impressed Marco by their royal demeanor—and by their wealth. This drawing from a sixteenth-century Indian album shows a prince putting a dancing elephant through its paces. The elephant wears a harness decorated with jangling bells and is led by a light-footed mahout. On its back kneels a fearful servant who hangs onto the saddle with his left hand.

TEXT CONTINUED FROM PAGE 130

In their devotion to an idol some parents dedicated a daughter to service in the temple of the idol. When the priests of the temple summoned these girls, they would come and entertain the idol by singing, dancing, playing on an instrument, or even tumbling. Several times a week a table covered with food was set in front of the idol, and while he was supposed to be eating, the girls sang and played for him. Then they themselves and the priests ate the food.

The legendary roc was pictured in The Arabian Nights *as strong enough to pick up three elephants.*

After passing through the Golconda diamond fields, famous for yielding some of the world's greatest diamonds, Marco came to a region noted for two of the most interesting castes, or groups, the Brahmans and the yogis. Marco describes the Brahmans as "the best and most honorable merchants in the world. Nothing could induce them to lie, even if their lives depended on it." They detested cheating, he says, and would help a stranger sell his goods without insisting on a profit for themselves. They hated all killing, and if any animal had to be slaughtered, they asked a Moslem to do it for them. They put much faith in signs and omens, allowing themselves to be influenced by the shadows they cast, by sneezes, and by the movements of tarantula spiders.

In the same northern region Marco saw the yogis, who were so fanatically religious that they denied themselves all worldly goods and comforts. "They go about stark naked," Marco relates, "saying that they are not ashamed of the state in which they were born." They worshiped the ox and wore a small image of it on their forehead. They used no plates but ate their food from dried leaves. Because they believed that all living things had souls, they would not kill anything, not even a worm or a louse. They not only refused to eat any slaughtered animal but any plant or root until it was completely dried. They drank nothing but water, fasted constantly, and did not mix with women. They slept naked in the open, with nothing under them.

The marvel was not that they did not die, Marco explains, but that they lived to a great old age. Although he was not an educated man, and may not always have appreciated the higher aspects of every culture, his treatment of the Brahmans and the yogis was remarkable for its tolerance and understanding, and its respect for strange beliefs.

Leaving India, the expedition made for its last port, in southern Persia. But before quitting the Indian Ocean, Marco adds as much information as he can about the places around it that he had heard about but had not visited. Here, occasionally, fancy interferes with fact, as in his tale of a tribe in which the men lived on an "island of males" while the women lived on a neighboring "island of females." The men visited the women only in the spring. This legend is much like that of the Amazons and was told about various tribes in different parts of the world. Another fantastic story is that of the roc, a bird supposedly found on Madagascar, which was so large and strong that it was said to be capable of carrying off an elephant. Surprisingly, fossil bones reveal that a huge bird did once live in Madagascar, but the "roc" that Marco describes was a legendary creature found only in such tales as that of Sinbad the Sailor in *The Arabian Nights*.

Living up to his promise in the prologue of his *Travels* to give "a description of the world"—meaning those parts of the world that Europeans knew nothing about—Marco devotes the last few chapters of his book to such northern lands as Siberia and Russia. Although he had never visited this area, which he calls the Land of Darkness, he gives much useful information about it, including descriptions of white bears, sables, and people who rode over frozen ground in sledges drawn by large dogs. He also reports that it was always dark there in the winter and always daylight in the summer.

Finally, after more than two years of tortuous voyaging through the southern seas, the convoy arrived in Persia. In his book Marco gives only one indication of how hard the journey was, how many accidents and storms, how many attacks of scurvy and other sickness, how much deadly heat, how much vile food and foul water they had endured: he tells us quite casually that all but eighteen of the six hundred passengers—not counting the crew—perished on the voyage.

MUSEO CIVICO, PADUA

On his final passage across the Arabian Sea, Marco may have sailed in a vessel rigged like this thirteenth-century merchant ship.

And then, after all their trials, the Polos learned that Arghun Khan, to whom they were bringing Princess Cocachin, had died. They were placed in a most perplexing situation, and for a while there seemed no solution for it. Then Ghazan, Arghun's grown son, solved their predicament by taking his father's place as the husband of the lovely princess.

The Polos remained nine months in Persia, resting from the ordeal of their journey. While there they received word that their friend Kublai Khan had died. Even as they mourned, they realized they had not left China a moment too soon. Then, after bidding farewell to Cocachin, who

BIBLIOTHEQUE NATIONALE, SERVICE PHOTOGRAPHIQUE

حکایت

توجه پادشاه اسلام بطرف شام و مصر و مصاف دادن
با مصریان و شکسته شدن ایشان و فتح ولایات شام

Two climactic events took place at the end of Marco's homeward trip: the marriage of Princess Cocachin to Ghazan Khan, and the death of Kublai. At left is a copy of an early fourteenth-century painting of Cocachin's wedding; at right is a scene of grief-stricken Mongols at the funeral bier of a ruler.

had grown so fond of Marco that she wept to see him go, the three men and their servants and slaves took to the caravan routes again.

They went first to Trebizond on the Black Sea and were surely pleased to see once again in the crowded streets the familiar faces of Genoese and Venetian traders. However, here in this bustling seaport, the Polos suffered a misfortune: judging from a passage found later in Maffeo's will, they lost a large amount of either money or goods. It appears that they were robbed, but of what and by whom it is not known.

From Trebizond they took ship again, sailing first to Constantinople and then out on the Aegean again, past the craggy tip of Greece, and up the Adriatic.

At last, in the year 1295, they came in sight of the graceful bell towers, the domes and gilded palaces, of Venice, framed by blue sky above and sparkling waters below. It is easy to imagine Marco's mixed feelings in that moment: the excitement at seeing again the city of his childhood and youth, and yet the pang at the premonition that the East, where he had spent twenty-four years filled with extraordinary and unforgettable experiences, was behind him forever.

He had left Venice as an unformed youth of seventeen; he returned to it a man of forty-one who had taken the longest journey in history and seen more of the world than any man of his time.

VIII

MARCO'S "MILLIONS"

PHOTO BY BOHM, VENICE

Marco does not tell what happened when the Polos, their servants, and their slaves, weatherbeaten and weary, came to the door of their home in the San Giovanni Chrisostomo district of Venice. But there are several stories that have been handed down for centuries. One of these relates that the Polos had "an indescribable something of the Tartar in their aspect and in their way of speech, having almost forgotten the Venetian tongue. Their garments were much the worse for wear, made of coarse cloth, and cut after the fashion of the Tartars." Much had changed, and as with Ulysses after his wanderings, or Rip Van Winkle after his long sleep, no one recognized them. How could the wife with whom Nicolo had lived so briefly twenty-five years before have recognized her husband in that bearded old man, or known her stepson in that sturdy figure in the Oriental robes? Had she not given them up for dead many years ago?

The legends recount that when the travelers began to relate their story to their friends and relatives—whom they themselves barely recognized—they were met with looks of doubt and disbelief. So the Polos arranged a banquet to which all their relatives were invited. The three travelers came to it dressed in the costliest satins, silks, and crimson damasks that they had brought back with them. While their guests watched in wonder they discarded these, left the room, and came back in the coarse, worn robes in which they had returned home. Like sorcerers in *The Arabian Nights*, they took off their garments and ripped open the seams and linings; out cascaded rubies, sapphires, emeralds, diamonds, and other precious gems, all of which

When they returned from China, the Polos entered their house through the gate above, all that remains of the original structure. At right is a religious procession showing the colorful costumes and buildings of Venice.

the Polos had sewed into their robes before they left China.

Whether or not their relatives and neighbors then believed more of their stories than they had before, tradition says that everyone began to treat them with much more respect and that Maffeo was even made a magistrate.

Appealing as this story may be, it is not entirely convincing. First, the Polos did not live like rich men after they returned, and Marco's will shows that he was only moderately well off. (Of course, he died almost thirty years after his return, and during that time he may have lost a good part of any fortune he had brought back.) If, moreover, the Polos did put on such a performance for their relatives and friends, it is curious that people still continued to think of many of Marco's stories as tall tales. Indeed, according to some sources he was popularly known as Marco of the Millions and the Polo house was called Millions' Court—names that supposedly refer to the numbers he was forever using in describing the wealth of China in general and of the Great Khan in particular. This attitude lingered on after he had died, and eventually the greatest traveler and the best reporter of his time became a figure in Venetian puppet shows—a comic character named *Il Milione*.

The fierce warfare between Venice and Genoa was waged on the open sea in battles like this. After one of the huge, many-oared ships (background) had rammed an opponent, sailors fought hand to hand.

DIREZIONE PALAZZO DUCALE, VENICE

The fact that Marco brought back such curiosities as yak wool, the dried head of a musk deer, a musk sac, sago, and the seeds of various plants should have helped convince doubters, but there are always those who prefer to make fun of anyone who shows up their ignorance.

Only in the past century, as scholars have studied Marco's book and explorers have followed in his path, has the accuracy of his reporting been generally accepted. When he does occasionally include a fantastic story, such as that of the men with tails, or a report of some miracle, he often adds that though he heard about it, he did not witness it himself.

More surprising are certain things he fails to mention—the Great Wall of China, tea drinking, eating with chopsticks, the binding of girls' feet, and printed books. But perhaps all of these became so familiar to him during the many years he lived in China that he did not realize how strange they might seem to outsiders.

One thing that had not changed while the Polos were away was the fierce trade rivalry between Venice and Genoa. Savage clashes between them took place constantly, especially on the high seas. In 1295 fleets sent out by the two cities almost wiped out each other's districts in Constantinople. As a merchant, Marco was inevitably drawn into the conflict and finally into a battle. One story is that he was in a fleet of fifteen Venetian galleys off the eastern Mediterranean coast when twenty-five Genoese merchant galleys attacked and overwhelmed them, capturing many Venetians, including Marco. Another story is that he was commander of a galley in a battle against the Genoese near the island of Curzola. In this engagement Marco is said to have bravely thrust his vessel into the forefront of the action, but the others did not follow, and the Venetians were badly defeated. According to this account, Marco was taken prisoner along with thousands of his countrymen.

N.Y. PUBLIC LIBRARY, RARE BOOK DIVISION

Genoa was called "the Superb" because of its excellent harbor and its mighty fleet. Marco may have been imprisoned in one of the towers visible in this 1486 woodcut.

Whichever story is correct, it is known that Marco was carried off to where "Genoa the Superb" perched proudly on a hillside above the Ligurian Sea. Although he was kept in a tower and not thrown into a foul dungeon with the common soldiers, it was a depressing and humiliating experience for one who had journeyed across a vast empire as the representative of the greatest monarch of his time. And yet in one way it proved a boon, for while in prison he had the leisure and the desire to dictate the book that was to make him forever famous.

It came about in this manner: to wile away the time,

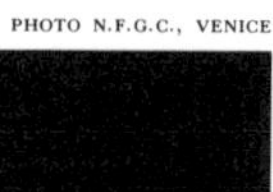
PHOTO N.F.G.C., VENICE

This vase is the only existing object thought to have been brought back from China by Marco. Though slightly cracked, the blue-glazed ceramic vessel is a perfect example of the artisanship of the period before the Mongol conquest.

Marco would tell his stories to his fellow prisoners, and later, as his reputation spread, to many leading citizens of Genoa who came to listen to him. One of those most impressed by his tales was a prisoner named Rustichello, who had been captured in Pisa when the Genoese had conquered and humbled that city in 1284. Rustichello had been a writer of romances, chiefly on such subjects as King Arthur and the Knights of the Round Table. He wrote in French so that educated men all over Europe might be able to read his works.

Listening to the vivid stories poured out by Marco, Rustichello saw an opportunity to write for once about the adventures of a flesh-and-blood hero instead of shadowy figures out of the past. Marco in turn welcomed the help of a professional writer in organizing and presenting the vast amount of information he had gathered. Once they had agreed to work together, Marco sent to his father in Venice for the notes he had taken in his travels. Although Rustichello's influence can be seen in the occasional use of the language of chivalry, especially in descriptions of battles, the book is that of a keen, practical-minded man giving a straightforward account of everything he has seen.

They had just finished the manuscript—in 1299—when Venice and Genoa concluded a truce, and the prisoners were released. After his years in jail, Marco returned to Venice once again. He was forty-five now, which in that day was considered past middle age. He had never married, although it is very possible he had taken a bride in China but had had to leave her behind. Now at last he took a wife, a certain Donata Badoer; all that is known of her is that she brought with her a good dowry. The couple had three daughters and several grandchildren, but no further descendants have been traced. At about the time of the

When he was released from prison, Marco came back to Venice for the last time. The site of his home is in the background, at center, of the detail below from a view of Venice—at the triangular junction of two of the city's many canals.

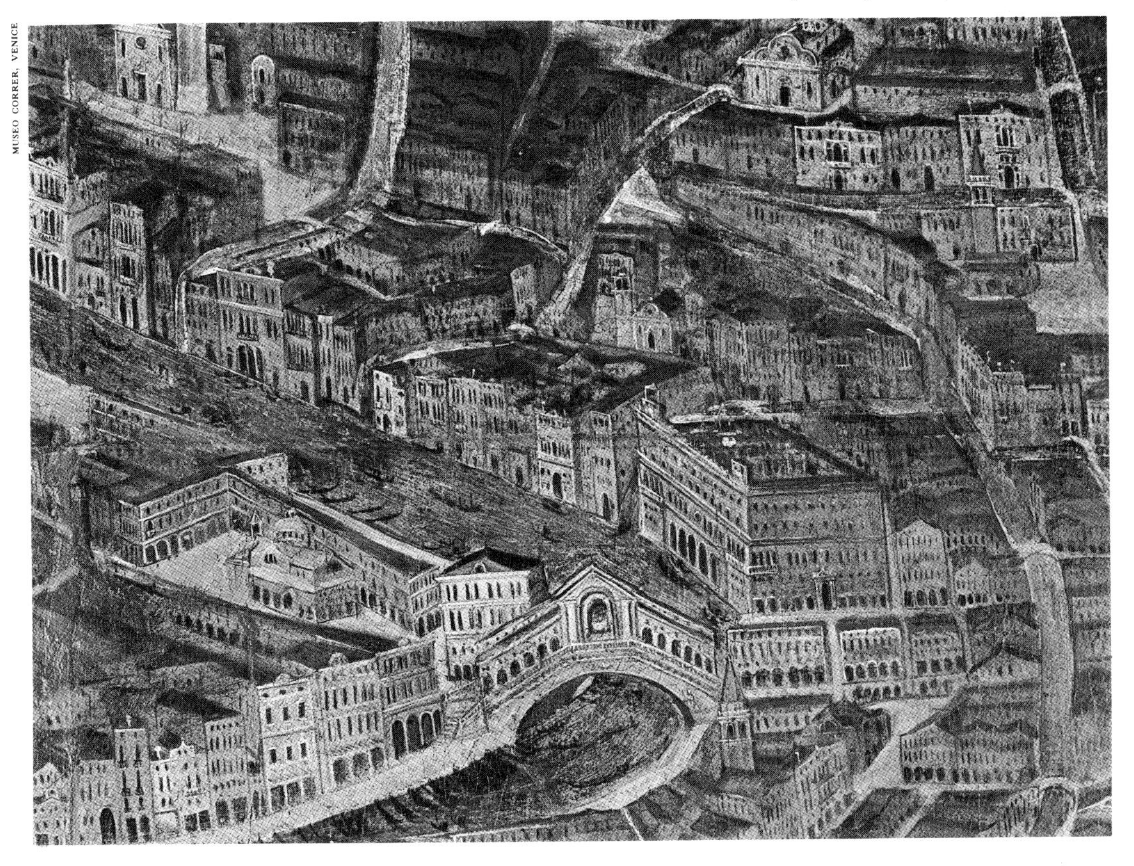

MUSEO CORRER, VENICE

marriage, Marco's father, Nicolo, the true pioneer in unknown lands, the man who had led Marco into the East and introduced him to the Great Khan, died in the fullness of his years.

In Venice, Marco resumed his trading activities, but life must have seemed dull and cramped after the splendor of the court at Khanbalik and the size and richness of Kinsai. Even though he traded with faraway Russia for furs and with England for tin and wool, and occasionally made arrangements for a shipload of pilgrims on their way to the Holy Land or sold Venetian mirrors to brides everywhere, it all soon became a humdrum routine. What could the cluster of ships in the harbor of Venice mean to one who had seen the forest of masts on the Yangtze? And what was the central market of the city compared to one in any of the ten great squares of Kinsai? Perhaps he dreamed from time to time of going back to China, but who would welcome and honor him now that Kublai was gone? And after a while it was too late.

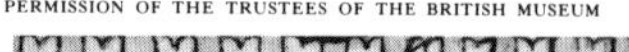
PERMISSION OF THE TRUSTEES OF THE BRITISH MUSEUM

Crowded stalls such as this were visited by many unfortunate Venetians who had to pawn their goods.

Others now ventured where Marco and his father and uncle had shown the way. For five or six more decades the caravan routes remained open, and missionaries and merchants made the journey to China. But the rulers there had changed. Where Kublai had been born a Mongol, with a Mongol's will to fight and conquer, his successors were born in China and acquired the Chinese distaste for war. As their will to rule grew weaker, Chinese rebelliousness became stronger. Finally, in 1371, the Chinese drove the Mongols out onto the steppes from which they had come.

But unlike the Mongols, who had been curious about foreigners and even protected the occasional visitor, the Chinese showed no tolerance toward strangers. They closed the door to the West, even exiling all foreigners. At the same time, raiding Turks began to disrupt the caravan routes across Asia. Trade waned, and the famous caravan cities dwindled. It would be a century and a half before the door was opened again, and then only wide enough to admit a few traders and an occasional missionary. So Marco's book was not only the first to pull aside the veil that hid the East but was one of the last for many years to come.

Since Marco was not a public official or a famous man whose activities would have been reported, most of what is known of his later years comes from the records of law courts. Because these court records are mainly about suits to recover money, a few of Marco's biographers have pictured him as having become greedy and quarrelsome—

GALLERIA ACCADEMIA, VENICE

Marco Polo's will (left) shows that although he could not leave his wife a fortune, he was able to provide for her. The document states that she would get an income for life plus certain furnishings, "including three beds . . ." It is dated January 9, 1324, one day after Marco's death, and is marked with the clerk's flower-like sign (lower left). Marco had been married when he was nearly fifty, older by far than the bridegroom in the Venetian wedding scene above.

BIBLIOTECA MARCIANA, VENICE

made bitter by the disbelief and mockery of his neighbors.

But some scholars had taken notice of his accounts. As soon as he brought the manuscript of his book back to Venice from the Genoa jail, copies of it were made in Latin and in several Italian dialects—for Venetians, Genoese, and Pisans could hardly understand each other in those days. During the next century the manuscript was translated into Spanish, German, Bohemian, Irish, and other languages. One hundred and thirty-eight copies of the manuscript have been found, one as recently as 1934. *The Travels of Marco Polo* circulated in manuscript form for almost 180 years before printed copies appeared in 1477, only 21 years after Johann Gutenberg invented movable type and produced the first printed book in Europe.

As he lay in his last illness, in January, 1324, Marco's thoughts must have wandered again and again to scenes from those far-past days on the caravan routes of Asia and in the empire of Kublai Khan: the bazaars of Bukhara, the jade in the stream beds of Khotan, the lovely dark-skinned women of Tunocain, the wild gorges of the Yangtze River, the azure and vermilion roof of the palace at Khanbalik, the courtiers in cloth of gold kneeling and bowing as the Great Khan emptied his golden goblet of wine.

Near the end, when the priest leaned over him and asked whether he wanted to take back some of the incredible stories he had told of what he had seen and done on his travels, Marco answered quietly, "I did not tell half of what I saw, for I knew I would not be believed."

After Marco's death, Venice prospered even more than in his life; increased trade with the lands of the East and the defeat of Genoa brought new wealth to the city. Venice at its height, around 1500, is seen in the stunning painting at left by Carpaccio. The first Italian book that included Marco's text appeared fifty-nine years later; the title page is shown at right.

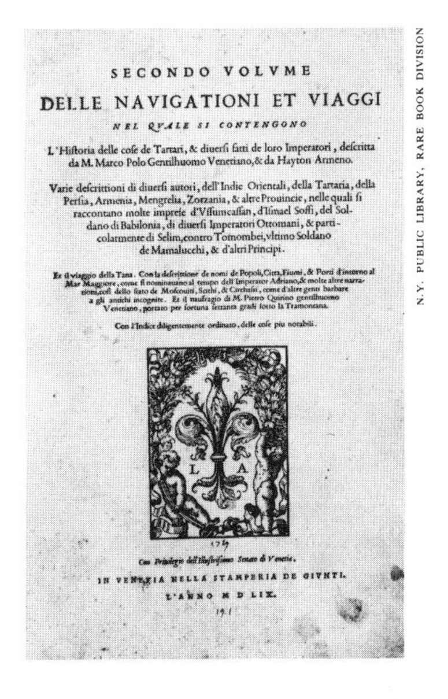

SECONDO VOLVME

DELLE NAVIGATIONI ET VIAGGI

NEL QVALE SI CONTENGONO

L'Historia delle cose de Tartari, & diuersi fatti de loro Imperatori, descritta da M. Marco Polo Gentilhuomo Venetiano, & da Hayton Armeno.

Varie descrittioni di diuersi autori, dell'Indie Orientali, della Tartaria, della Persia, Armenia, Mengrelia, Zorzania, & altre Prouincie, nelle quali si raccontano molte imprese d'Vssumcassan, d'Ismael Soffi, del Soldano di Babilonia, di diuersi Imperatori Ottomani, & particolarmente di Selim, contro Tomombei, vltimo Soldano de Mamalucchi, & d'altri Principi.

Et il viaggio della Tana. Con la descrittione de nomi de Popoli, Citta, Fiumi, & Porti d'intorno al Mar Maggiore, come si nominauano al tempo dell'Imperator Adriano, & molte altre narrationi, cosi dello stato de Moscouiti, Scithi, & Circhassi, come d'altre genti barbare a gli antichi incognite. Et il naufragio di M. Pietro Quirino gentilhuomo Venetiano, portato per fortuna settanta gradi sotto la Tramontana.

Con l'Indice diligentemente ordinato, delle cose piu notabili.

L A

Con Priuilegio dell'Illustrissimo Senato di Venetia.

IN VENETIA NELLA STAMPERIA DE GIVNTI.

L'ANNO M D LIX.

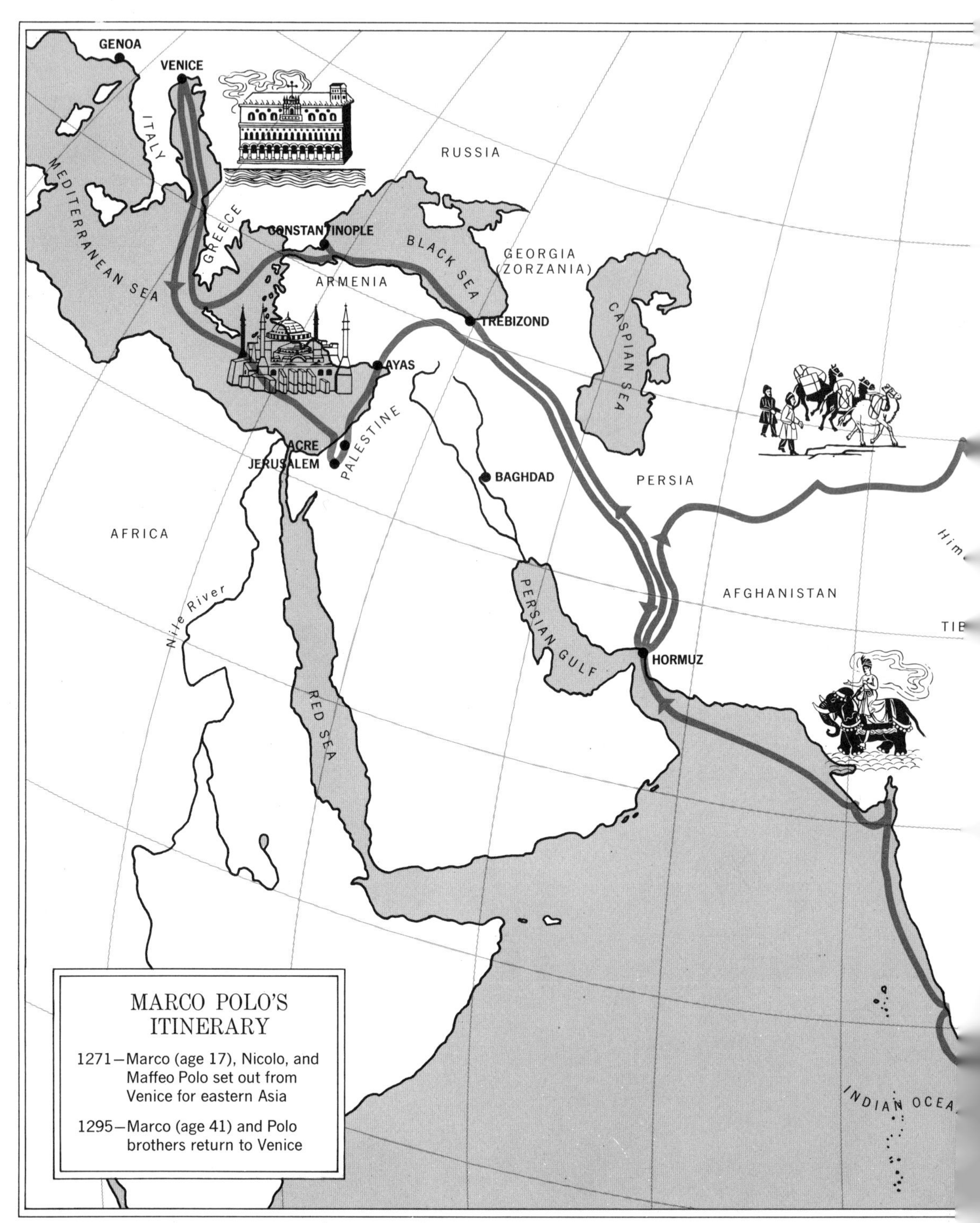

The extent of Marco Polo's travels may be seen in this map of his

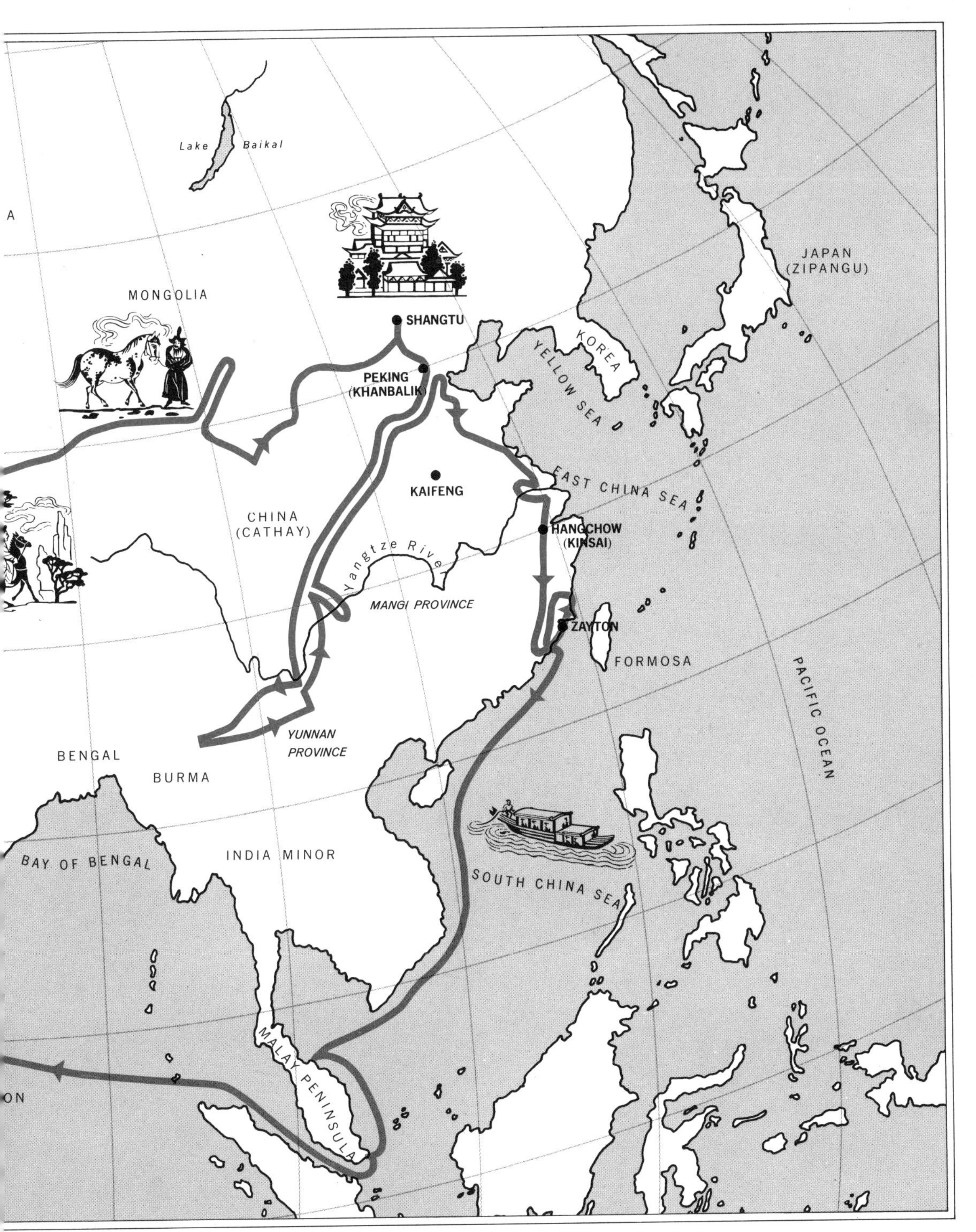

e route across most of the land and water areas of the Eastern world.

ACKNOWLEDGMENTS

The Editors are deeply indebted to the staff members of many private and public collections in which paintings, photographs, and articles of special importance to this book were found. Foremost among these collections are the National Palace Museum, Taichung, Taiwan (China); the New York Public Library; The Metropolitan Museum of Art, New York; the Bibliothèque Nationale, Paris; and the British Museum, London. In addition, the Editors wish to thank the following individuals and organizations for their assistance and for making available material in their collections:

Dr. Aschwin Lippe, Associate Curator in charge of Far Eastern Art, Metropolitan Museum of Art

Dr. James Cahill, Curator of Chinese Art, Freer Gallery of Art, Washington, D.C.

Dr. Richard Ettinghausen, Head Curator, Near Eastern Art, Freer Gallery of Art

Lewis M. Stark, Mrs. Maud Cole, and Mrs. Philomena Houlihan, Rare Book Division, New York Public Library

Chinese News Service, New York

Prof. Tullia Gasparrini Leporace, Director, Biblioteca Nazionale Marciana, Venice

Prof. Giovanni Mariacher, Director, Museo Correr, Venice

Dr. Alessandro Bettagno, Secretary, Istituto di Storia dell'Arte Fondazione Giorgio Cini, Venice

Mlle. T'Sersteven, Assistant Curator, Musée Guimet, Paris

Marcel Thomas, Chief Curator, Cabinet des Manuscrits, Bibliothèque Nationale

Department of Oriental Antiquities, British Museum

Department of Oriental Printed Books and Manuscripts, British Museum

Special research: Italy—Maria Todorow, Lina Urban; France—Claire de Forbin; England—Susanne Puddefoot; Spain—Jane Horton de Cabanyes

Maps by Herbert Borst

This engraving of Marco Polo in old age is from a 1600 painting.

FURTHER REFERENCE

Readers interested in further examining the art and artifacts of the medieval period of the Far East will find collections of varying kinds in the following museums in the United States: the Smithsonian Institution, Freer Gallery of Art, Washington, D.C.; China Institute in America, Asia House, and The Metropolitan Museum of Art, New York City; Philadelphia Museum of Art; Museum of Fine Arts, Boston; Art Institute of Chicago; William Rockhill Nelson Gallery of Art, Kansas City; Cleveland Museum of Art; Denver Art Museum; and the Fine Arts Society of San Diego.

For those who wish to read more about Marco Polo and the places he visited, the following books are recommended:

Cahill, James. *Chinese Painting*. Skira, 1960.

Collis, Maurice. *Marco Polo*. New Directions Books, 1960.

Dawson, Christopher, Ed. *The Mongol Mission*. Sheed and Ward, 1955.

Gernet, Jacques. *Daily Life in China on the Eve of the Mongol Invasion*. George Allen & Unwin Ltd., 1962.

Goodrich, L. Carrington. *A Short History of the Chinese People*. Harper & Brothers, 1959.

Grousset, Rene. *The Rise and Splendour of the Chinese Empire*. University of California Press, 1953.

Hart, Henry H. *Venetian Adventurer*. Stanford University Press, 1947.

Hudson, G. F. *Europe and China*. Beacon Press, 1961.

Moule, A. C. *Quinsai with Other Notes on Marco Polo*. Cambridge University Press, 1957.

Olschki, Leonard. *Marco Polo's Asia*. University of California Press, 1960.

Reischauer, Edwin O., and Fairbank, John K. *East Asia, the Great Tradition*. Houghton Mifflin, 1960.

Rugoff, Milton, Ed. *The Travels of Marco Polo*. Signet Classics, 1961.

Runciman, Steven. *A History of the Crusades*. Vol. III. Cambridge University Press, 1955.

Sickman, Laurence, and Soper, Alexander. *The Art and Architecture of China*. Penguin Books, 1956.

Spieser, Werner. *The Art of China*. Crown Publishers, 1960.

Yule, Sir Henry. *The Book of Ser Marco Polo*. Scribner, 1903.

INDEX

Bold face indicates pages on which maps or illustrations appear

L

M

N

O

P

R

S

T

U

V

W

Y

Z

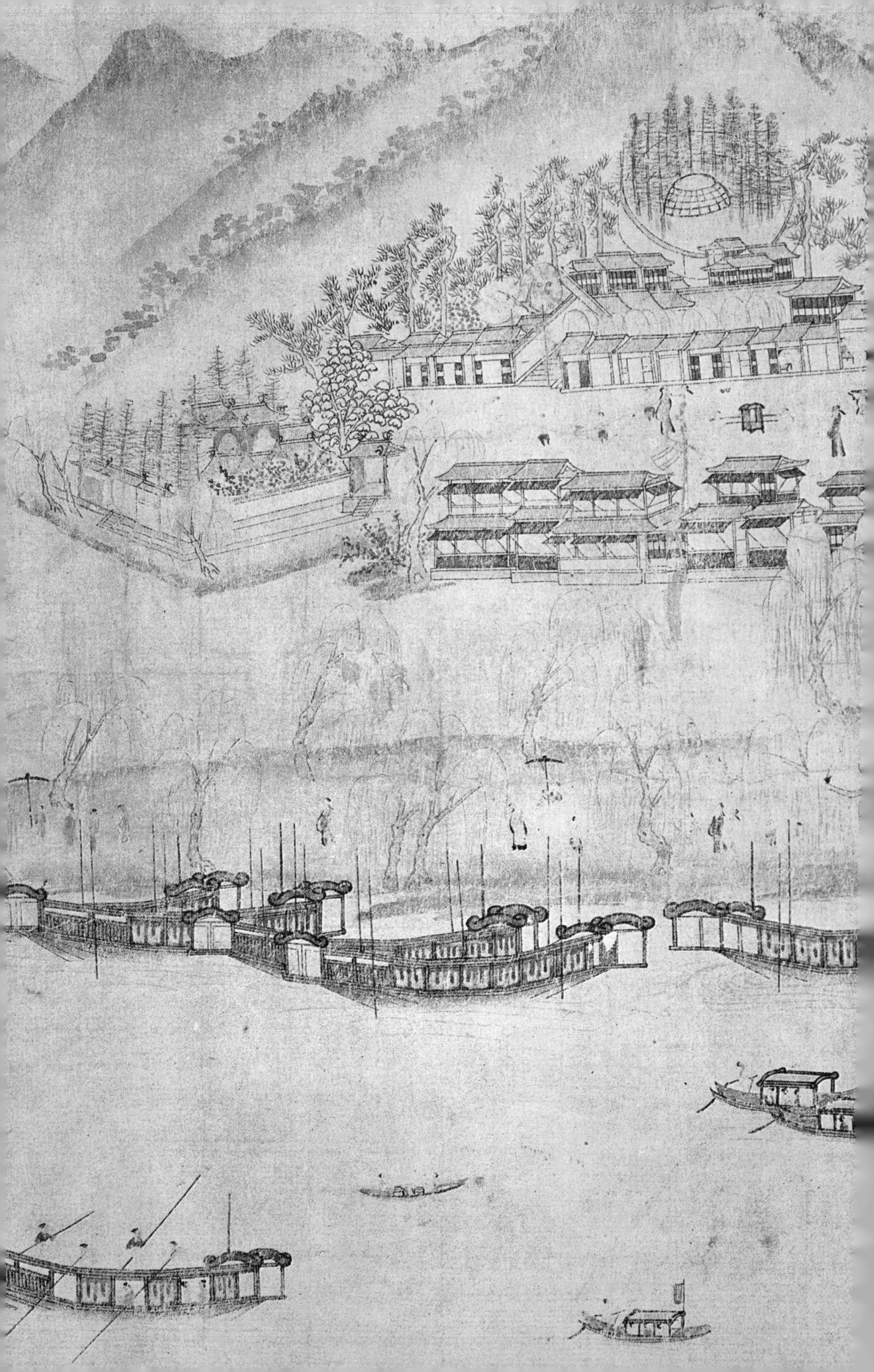